Praise for T[he Lotion Book]

"*The Lotion Book* is a revitalizing, inspiring and practical book that offers readers a plan to reclaim their lives."
  Bernadette R. Anderson, MD, Founder of Life in Harmony
  RefocusingYou.org

"*The Lotion Book* is like a conversation with one of your best girlfriends. Dr. Townsend reminds us that 'self-care is not selfish'—and for that I am so GRATEFUL!"
  Daphney Thomas, Founder & CEO of CoaCoa Goddess
  CoaCoaGoddess.com

"Dr. Townsend has been in all of our heads; written our very thoughts; shared all of our secrets; and sits in the room, smiling, as we turn the pages, answering the questions, and musing through the 'joys of our lives.'"
  Carol J. Hinton, CEO of YWCA Dayton

"Dr. Townsend's delightful and heartfelt story challenges women to retire their 'capes' and take much needed time to bring balance to their lives."
  LaTonya Branham, author of *CultureSeek*
  LaTonyaBranham.com

"*The Lotion Book* succinctly and humorously examines a challenge for all women: finding **TiME**. Dr. Townsend challenges us to ditch the self-imposed (and other-imposed) guilt that prevents us from making ourselves a priority."
  Millie L. Chamberlin, Ph.D., Retired Educator

"I found this book to be a wonderful resource to find ways to take **TiME** to care for myself."
  Anna Magnusson, Director of Donor Relations Advancement
  Wright State University

"Dr. Townsend interjects humor into her writing about a topic that is changing who women are as much as the waves of the feminist movement."
>Linda Blum, School Board President
>Northmont City Schools

"*The Lotion Book* is foundational inspiration for women across the globe! Thank you, Dr. Townsend, for leading the way to help us all lotion up!"
>Sarah Israel, Diamond Executive of Soul Purpose
>NaturesOuterBeauty.net

"*It All Started When I Stopped Using Lotion* made me take a look at my life. I saw that I needed to make some changes ASAP. What a great book!"
>Sonya L. Taylor-Allison, Factory Worker

"This book changed my life! When I read *The Lotion Book*, I said, 'Wow! Is there a hidden camera in my purse?' Dr. Townsend painted a vivid picture of my frenzied life and then…showed me how to make **TiME** for myself to turn my chaos into calm."
>Tamala Moore, High School Counselor

"Learning how Dr. Townsend took her personal journey from chaos to calm has motivated me to do the same."
>Jeanne Porter, President of Women in Business Networking
>WomenInBusinessNetworking.com

"Dr. Townsend provides eminently practical advice that affirms, guides, directs and positively influences those who are missing balance in their lives."
>Quincy Taylor, Independent Mary Kay Sales Director

It All Started When I Stopped Using Lotion: One Woman's Journey From Chaos to Calm

By

Karen M. R. Townsend, Ph.D.

Published by

Queen V Publishing
Dayton, Ohio
QueenVPublishing.com

Published by

Queen V Publishing
Dayton, Ohio
QueenVPublishing.com

Copyright © 2011 by Karen M.R. Townsend, Ph.D.

All rights reserved. No part of this book may be reproduced or transmitted in any form or by any means, electronic or mechanical, without prior written consent of the Publisher, except for the inclusion of brief quotes in a review.

Queen V Publishing is a contract publishing company of standard and integrity. We allow the message in you to do what it was sent to do for others.

Library of Congress Control Number: 2011905196

ISBN-13: 978-0-9817436-5-3

Cover design by Candace K
Author photo by Mitchell Stanford
Edited by Valerie J. Lewis Coleman of PenOfTheWriter.com

Printed in the United States of America

Dedication

To my daughters:

Syron and KaeLyn,

May you always take **TiME** to put on lotion!

All my love,
Mama

Table of Contents

Preface 9
Acknowledgements 11
Journal Entries 15
Introduction 17
Chaos 19
No Time for Lotion 21
Take Your TiME! 25
The Journey Begins 27
Check Your TiME 31
A Journey Back in TiME 35
How Are You $pending Your TiME? 41
Seven Steps for Restoring Balance to Your Life ... 47
   Step One: Do Not Disturb 49
   Step Two: Joy! 57
   Step Three: Build a Chaos to Calm Team 67
   Step Four: Just Say, "No!" 75
     KT's 10-Step Decision Making Process 84
   Step Five: Just Say, "Yes!" 85
   Step Six: PMS - It's Not What You Think! 91
   Step Seven: 52 Ways to Take Your TiME 97
Final Thoughts 113
Next Steps: Opportunities to Apply Lotion 115
About the Author 121
Training and Consulting 122
Queen V Publishing 123

Preface

Long before this book was written, I knew that the title would be *It All Started When I Stopped Using Lotion*.

It struck me as a pretty catchy title and I figured that if the book became popular and really took off, I could secure a major lotion company to sponsor my book tour.

As the writing progressed, I considered a few other titles; however, when I tested the other options among family, friends and colleagues, the responses could be categorized as mediocre, polite, less-than-enthusiastic and at best, lukewarm. But whenever I said, "I'm thinking about titling the book *It All Started When I Stopped Using Lotion*," I received one of two responses: 1) hysterical laughter or 2) a look of bewilderment followed by "What is that going to be about?"

Any writer will tell you that an inquiry into what a book is about indicates interest. If uncontrollable emotion (i.e. laughter) is expressed, then you've got them hooked. The decision to opt for the title—which I lovingly refer to as *The Lotion Book*—came easy for me.

So, what is this book about? Well, while the title may incite a chuckle, the subject *is not* a laughing matter. Women get so caught up in doing for others, that we often stop doing the little things—like putting on lotion—for ourselves. Why? Because we convince ourselves that we don't have the time, not realizing that giving up the little things often begins a pattern of self-neglect. We give up one thing, then another, then another, then another....

After months and months of not using lotion, I finally came to my senses. I realized that not only was my skin in need of moisture, but my life was in desperate need of balance.

How about you? When you think about your life as it is now, are you living in a state of perpetual calm? If so, then kudos to you! Or are you like countless other busy, working women—living a life filled with chaos? If you fall into the latter category, then this book is for you!

It All Started When I Stopped Using Lotion is an account of my personal journey from chaos to calm. After suffering in silence for far too long and struggling to regain balance in my own life, I figured out that no one solution could free me from chaotic living. And while I thought I was the only one trying to figure out how to keep all the balls in the air, I discovered that other women were juggling, I mean, struggling, too.

My hope is that you might recognize yourself in me and find one, two, three or seven strategies that will move you from chaos to calm!

Here's to chaos-free living!

Karen

Acknowledgements

Anyone who has ever written a book already knows this, and anyone who aspires to write a book needs to know this: No one writes a book alone.

First and foremost, I must acknowledge God and His awesome power in this entire process. While the idea for this book was born years ago, not until I surrendered all was I able to really get to work on this project. Proverbs 3:6 reminds us "In all your ways acknowledge Him, and He shall direct thy paths." Amen!

Next, I must acknowledge my husband, Sylvester, and my two daughters, Syron and KaeLyn.

For twenty-plus years, Sylvester has stood by my side and supported me in everything I have ever wanted to do. He has allowed me to pursue my dreams, been my biggest cheerleader and kept me grounded whenever it appeared that I might be caught up with my own PR. I am confident he loves me. How do I know? Because when he read the title of this book, he said, "Baby, if I had known you needed lotion, I would have bought you some!" What a man! My man! Please know that I love you!

My daughters: As I struggled to finish this book, both girls offered their own brand of encouragement.

My oldest, Syron, said, "These women don't need an epic, Mommy. Just finish the book!"

Message received and acknowledged.

My youngest, KaeLyn, who has an uncanny sense of knowing when her mommy is stressed, once encouraged me to extend a business trip and "…stay a few extra days in California."

At their young ages, these little women wanted me to finish this book for you! I love you, girls!

I also have to acknowledge:

- Lucy Reynolds, my mother, for instilling in me a love for books at an early age. When she *forced me* as a third grader to participate in the public library's summer reading program, who knew that one day I would have a book to contribute to the library? Thanks, Mama, for creating a reader…and a writer!
- Etene Terrell, who—in addition to being a busy, working woman, wife and mother of three—is my sister. Our lives are often so busy that sometimes the only time we get to talk is during our evening commutes around 5:30 PM. Our daily conversation often goes like this:

  "How are you doing?"

  "Tired!"

  "Me, too!"

  Thanks for never being too busy or too tired to encourage me.
- Brenda Cochran: Whether she realizes it, she was the impetus for this book. Brenda is a reporter for The Dayton (Ohio) Weekly News. Some years ago, she did a story on me following a presentation that I made for the YWCA's Professional Women Lecture Series. At the conclusion of the program, Brenda asked, "So when is the book coming out?" Well, Brenda, I can finally say

that the book is finished, but it never would have been started without you.

- Rev. Dr. LaCreta Clark: My sisterfriend who provided a platform for me to test market my first *Take Your **TiME*** presentation. The inaugural event occurred at Wilberforce University when she was Assistant Dean of Students. Although LaCreta now lives in Michigan, she still remains close to my heart.
- Donna Audette, former CEO of the YWCA Dayton (and current Director of Programs for the American Red Cross in New Mexico), for the invitation all those years ago to share my Take Your **TiME** philosophy with the women of our community.
- My angel investors: Leesa Baker (CEO, YWCA Piqua, Ohio), Penny Brown, Rose Burnett, Jacqueline Johnson, Valerie Shaw and Fawn Williams. These ladies pre-ordered this book before it was finished. Talk about faith! Every time I wanted to abandon the book, I thought about the women who had expressed their faith in me and that kept me committed to completion. I appreciate your $upport and patien¢e more than you know.
- The Power Ladies: Andi, Adrienne, Fawn, Toni, Rolnecia and Wanda. Regardless of what is going on in my life, these six women are always there to encourage and support me—whether with pompoms to cheer me on or tissue to dry my tears. Ladies, after a looooonnnnggg delay, we can finally chill the champagne and celebrate our latest book.
- LeRoy White: When you asked, "Whatcha' waiting for?" I really had to think about it. And because I had no reasonable response, I had to stop procrastinating and start writing. Thanks for "getting on my nerves" so that I would get this book done.

- Sabrina Dean: When it was crunch time and I publically announced that I was committed to finishing my book before the end of 2010, Ms. Dean took it upon herself to send me a message every Monday. The text simply read, "I can't wait to read your book!" Well Sabrina, I really didn't think you were going to text me every week. The wait is finally over.
- My ProTrack classmate and fellow NSA Ohio member, Greg Kozera: When I asked you to call me periodically and check on my progress, I really didn't think you would do it! Geez, I mean, thanks!
- The Dayton Daily News (DDN): Many years ago, DDN offered advance publicity for my book. It has been so long ago, I don't even know if the archives still exist. So for all those who read the DDN article and were looking forward to reading my book, here it is.

And last, but certainly not least...
- Valerie J. Lewis Coleman: By far, the best writing coach, editor and publisher in the world! I truly appreciate your patience, encouragement, words of wisdom and unwavering faith in me. I hope you are proud of what we have done! Whether we make it to "the couch" (and you know whose couch I'm talking about), I am confident that this book will influence the lives of many women! Queen V, I love you, girl!

It All Started When I Stopped Using Lotion

Journal Entries

Wednesday, November 18, 2009
4:37 PM
I just finished yelling at my fifteen-year-old daughter. And while she may or may not have deserved it, my outburst of emotion was an aha moment for me.

In the nine years since I started writing *The Lotion Book*, so much has happened. I "retired" from my job, completed a Ph.D., launched a training-and-consulting business and developed a series of personal empowerment programs for women promoted on my website **AboutMySisters.com**.

Yes, I have been busy and I have been in chaos. Perhaps that's why I struggled to finish the book.

Even with the encouragement of family and friends, the anticipation and requests to purchase from potential readers, book pre-sales by groups of women and offers to promote the book once finished, I still struggled to finish it.

Then it hit me: I have not yet finished this book because to publish such a work at this stage in my life would be hypocritical.

~ ~ ~ ~

When I was growing up, my mother listened to BB King. She loved this blues artist and one of his songs in particular stands out in my mind. In 1974, he had a hit song titled *I'd Like to Live the Love That I Sing About*. While the lyrics spoke of love and tenderness, the singer seemed to be conflicted. It was as though the words of the song were out of sync with the life he was living. Just as the lyrics didn't accurately reflect his life, neither do the words I have been writing.

I'd like to live the life that I write about in my book.

I know what it takes to live a joyful, balanced and chaos-free life. I give speeches, conduct workshops and host women's conferences and retreats to teach these principles. But for some reason, I haven't been living the life that I write about. So maybe, just maybe, this contradiction is why I've been at this book for so long.

Well, rest assured, I get it now. And because I get it, soon you will get it, too—the book that is!

December 1, 2010
The book is finished. I finally figured out how to live the life I have been writing about…for ten long years!

Enjoy!

It All Started When I Stopped Using Lotion

Introduction

I have always loved to take bubble baths. When I was a little girl, I enjoyed making pretend ice cream cones from the bubbles. When I got my first real job out of graduate school, my bubble baths were a daily indulgence to wash away the stress of the day. Once I got married, my husband became accustomed to my nightly retreats to the bathroom. As an expectant mother, my bubble baths soothed my ever-expanding belly. Once I became a mom, my evening baths were a treat to myself: thirty to forty-five minutes of uninterrupted time when I focused all my attention on ME!

After my evening bubble bath, a ritual ensued. First, I slathered my body with moisture-rich lotion and then I slipped on my softest, cuddliest jammies. If it was cold outside, I might put on a pair of socks to keep my feet warm and make a cup of hot chocolate. My evenings often ended with me curling up with a good book and then preparing for bed. One day, however, my nightly ceremony changed forever. And as clearly as I can recall, it all started when I stopped using lotion…

Karen M. R. Townsend, Ph.D.

It All Started When I Stopped Using Lotion

Part One

Chaos

Karen M. R. Townsend, Ph.D.

It All Started When I Stopped Using Lotion

No Time for Lotion

Every busy, working mom can relate to my typical weekday: I arrive home from my day job. You know, like the one you work from 7 to 3, 8 to 4 or 9 to 5, and then I start my second job. First, I try to locate my children. Are they home? At the neighbor's house? Or, Heaven forbid, have I forgotten to pick them up from ballet, gymnastics, Girl Scouts, choir or soccer?

No, they are at home. Whew! And when they hear me close the front door, they bound down the stairs and ask, "What's for dinner?"

Oh, yes! Dinner. I look in the fridge to find something that will qualify as a nutritiously sound meal. What about PB & J with frozen broccoli? The children accept the culinary delight, but my husband—well, that's a different story.

Once I get a handle on the dinner situation, the homework battle begins. Does my daughter's fourth-grade teacher really expect me to remember how to divide fractions? I try my best to help my daughter with her homework, but every time I ask her if she understands what to do, she says, "Mommy, let's wait until *Sponge Bob Square Pants* is over."

Oh, fine! I'll just do the homework myself!

Okay, let's review. Dinner is done. Homework is done. Now, it's time for baths. Yes! A warm, luxurious, relaxing bubble bath. Oh, I forgot. The bath that I'm running is not for me, it's for my daughter.

What I wouldn't give to strip down to my birthday suit and jump in. *Calgon, take me away!*

While I would give my left Jimmy Choo pump to get in the bathtub, I have to fight with my daughters to get them to bathe. In the process of this battle royale, my face gets wet, my hair gets wet and my brand new business suit gets wet!

Hey! Why in the world am I still wearing a business suit at 8:30 in the evening?

Once both girls are out of the tub, lotioned and in their jammies, I read them a bedtime story. A few minutes later, the sounds of peaceful slumber echo through the room. No, it's not one of the girls…it's me! Have you ever fallen asleep while reading a bedtime story? I'm pretty sure that it's not supposed to work that way.

At 9:30, I sit to rest for the first time since I walked in the front door four hours earlier. The sad part is…I am sitting on the toilet.

When I wake up twenty minutes later, I decide that it is time for me to take my bath. Even though I am exhausted, I add bubbles to the water and attempt to relax a few minutes. Once I get out of the bathtub, I skip the lotion. That would just take too much time.

The next four evenings were each replays of the day before (i.e. activities, homework, dinner, etc.) except for one difference: not only did I skip the lotion, I also skipped the bath. I took showers because baths just take too much time.

Skipping the lotion and exchanging baths for showers seemed like insignificant changes, but little did I know, these simple modifications would have far-reaching effects; effects that went unnoticed for three months.

It All Started When I Stopped Using Lotion

My girlfriend, Jacquie, and I decided to treat ourselves to a day at the spa. I got the full treatment: facial, massage, manicure, catered lunch and the final indulgence of my day—a pedicure. I shared with the pedicurist that I had developed a callous down the center of my left foot.

When I pulled my foot out of the soaking tub, he examined it and then asked, "Do you do a lot of walking?"

"Yes, but I have always walked a lot."

"How often do you wear high heels?"

"Every day, but I have worn high heels every day for years."

"When you take baths, do you use a pumice stone to smooth your feet?"

"When I take baths? A bath? Why, I don't take baths anymore. I just don't have the time."

As funny as it may sound, at that moment, I reflected on the last three months of my life. Never before had I been more stressed; more impatient; more angry. I no longer took the time to get my hair done at the salon. I no longer took the time to polish my fingernails and toenails on Sunday evenings. Since it was autumn, I no longer took the time to shave my legs or underarms on a regular basis.

While soaking my feet in a tub at a posh spa, I realized that I no longer took *time for me!* And it all started when I stopped using lotion!

First, I stopped using lotion.
Then I stopped taking baths.
Then I stopped shaving my legs.
Then I stopped shaving my underarms.
Then I stopped going to the beauty salon.
Then I stopped doing my nails.
Then I developed a callous on the bottom of my foot.

Before I realized what had happened, I stopped being patient, loving and kind.

On that brisk October day, as the pedicurist worked to smooth out the hardened skin on the bottom of my left foot, I made a commitment to change. I owed it to myself to take care of ME.

In addition to taking care of those around me, my schedule had to change to include time for ME. I vowed to start taking baths again and…start using lotion!

It All Started When I Stopped Using Lotion

Part Two

Take Your TiME!

Karen M. R. Townsend, Ph.D.

It All Started When I Stopped Using Lotion

The Journey Begins

Some years ago, I functioned more like a robot than a human. My life was completely out of balance and I was in constant motion as a wife and working mother with two small children. I had a full-time job, a part-time consulting practice and I was completing my Ph.D. Not to mention the four boards on which I served, church activities to which I committed and the sorority functions I attempted to attend.

In all that I was doing for my family, career and community, little time was left for me. That's when I came up with the concept of "Take Your **TiME**."

"Take Your **TiME**" began as a workshop for busy, working women who were overwhelmed, overextended and overly preoccupied with the needs of everyone else. The workshop—and this book—were based on seven simple strategies designed to help women regain balance.

When people inquired about the workshop, they thought that "**TiME**" was a typographical error.

"No, it is not a typo," I said with authority. "The spelling is indeed correct."

The unique spelling of "**TiME**" was intentional. It serves as a visual reminder that as busy, working women, we need to regularly and consistently take time for ME. I admit that this task is easier said than done. And I can recall one instance when this mandate caused me to do some serious introspection.

I had conducted the "Take Your **TiME**" workshop several times around Dayton, Ohio (my current home), when I received an invitation from the local YWCA to present an abbreviated version for its Professional Women's Lecture Series. I was flattered! What a wonderful opportunity to share my expertise. I planned to share my wisdom on how it is not only possible, but *necessary* for women to take time for themselves. And what better person to serve as a role model than me? Not!

As the date for the lecture drew closer, I felt more like a hypocrite with each passing day. A little voice inside my head said, *Who are you to tell anyone how to balance their life, especially when yours is so totally out of balance?* Truth be told, I burned the candle at both ends. And unbeknownst to the public, I was getting burned more often than I cared to admit.

Thank God for life's little cheerleaders. I shared my anxiety with a colleague whose comforting words made it possible for me to move forward and prepare for the lecture.

After sharing my concerns and fears, her response was simple yet profound. She said, "Karen, you teach best what you most need to learn."

Well, I was destined to be a great teacher, because Heaven knew that this was a lesson I, too, needed to learn! Years later, those words still resonate with me. They reassured me that not only could I conduct the presentation, but that I would eventually learn the lesson I had been asked to teach.

I didn't have all the answers then, I don't have all the answers now and I will probably never have all the answers.

It All Started When I Stopped Using Lotion

But I want to share strategies with you that I know will work...if only you take the **TiME** to work them.

Karen M. R. Townsend, Ph.D.

It All Started When I Stopped Using Lotion

Check Your TiME

Before we begin, let's take an assessment of your **TiME**.

From the choices listed below, put a check next to the statement that best describes your current use of **TiME**. Remember **TiME** means "**Time for ME!**"

    A. _____ I have all the **TiME** I need.

    B. _____ I need **TiME** on a regular basis.

    C. _____ I need more **TiME**.

    D. _____ I need some **TiME**. I don't have any.

    E. _____ **TiME**? What is **TiME** and how do I get some?

If you checked A, give yourself four points.
If you checked B, give yourself three points.
If you checked C, give yourself two points.
If you checked D, give yourself one point.
And if you checked E, keep reading!

Actually, you should keep reading regardless of how you answered because if we are truly honest, we all need more **TiME**.

Do you ever stop to think about all the things you have to do in any given day? All the hats you have to wear. All the responsibilities that you have to meet.

Well, I thought about it. And as a result of the epiphany of not having time left for ME, I decided to challenge my thinking. You know, thinking that I had to do everything for everyone else and once I was done, then and only then, could I attempt to do things that were important to me. Thinking that says if I multi-task, I can be more effective and efficient. Thinking that led me to believe that if I stayed up later or got up earlier, one day I would catch up. This mode of thinking was totally and completely WRONG! Contrary to popular belief, I was not, nor have I ever been, Superwoman. So, on that day, I retired my cape and decided to do things differently.

What about you? Are you trying to do it all? As a busy, working woman, are you the woman I used to be? Attempting to run your home, business, family and career all by yourself—never asking for assistance? Are you like me—a woman who burned the candle at both ends and the middle? Be warned: sooner rather than later, you are probably going to burn out!

Studies reveal that for the first time in history, women are closing the gap with men and not just as it applies to wages and salaries. I celebrate our advances in those areas. When it comes to medical conditions like hypertension and heart disease, women are catching up with men and in some cases, surpassing them. What's the number one cause of death for men? Heart disease. What's the number one cause of death for women? Heart disease.

According to information from the American Heart Association's 2009 *Heart Disease and Stroke Statistics*, more women die from heart disease, stroke and other cardiovascular diseases than men. Let me tell you, that is one gender race I have no desire to win. As if that weren't enough bad news, more than one in three women has some

It All Started When I Stopped Using Lotion

form of cardiovascular disease. One in three! Most women are not even aware that they are at risk.

Many years ago, during my freshman orientation, a college administrator attempted to make a point about retention. He said, "Look to your left. Now look to your right. By the end of the year, one of you won't be here."

Sadly, I could make that same statement today as it applies to women and heart disease. If I stood before you giving a presentation, I might say, "Look to your left. Now look to your right. Chances are one of you has cardiovascular disease."

Actually, I qualify as the one in three with cardiovascular disease. In 2010, I was diagnosed with left ventricular hypertrophy. Since I don't have any of the typical risk factors associated with this diagnosis (i.e. high blood pressure, diabetes, weight issues), one possible explanation is stress. For this reason alone, moving from chaos to calm was imperative not only to my health, but to my life!

Today's women are doing more personally and professionally than ever before, but at what cost?

Oprah Winfrey put it best when she said, "You can have it all. You just can't have it all at once."

Yes, you can be every woman, as Chaka Khan told us decades ago. You just can't be *every* woman *every* day!

Now, more than ever, it is important for you to take your **TiME**.

Karen M. R. Townsend, Ph.D.

It All Started When I Stopped Using Lotion

A Journey Back in TiME

    Several years ago, my family—seven adults and six children—took a trip to Disney World. Since we live in Ohio, we flew to Florida.
    I have traveled by airplane many times; however, for the first time that I could remember, I actually listened to the safety instructions. Not because I was so concerned for my own safety, but rather I was concerned about the safety of my traveling companions. I guess I wanted to make sure that I knew what to do in the event of an emergency.
    If you have ever flown, then you know the standard drill. The captain's voice comes over the PA system. She welcomes you on board, confirms the destination and then informs you of the length of the flight.
    The flight attendants indicate the locations of the restrooms, point out the emergency exits and then say, "In the unlikely event of a sudden change in cabin pressure, an oxygen mask will fall from the compartment above your head. If you are traveling with small children or someone who needs assistance, put your mask on first and then assist them with theirs."
    What?

Karen M. R. Townsend, Ph.D.

I had heard those instructions dozens of times before, but this time, as I sat between my two daughters—who were twenty-three-months and six-years old—I *heard* them. Did the airline really expect me to take care of myself and then take care of my babies? They must be mad! My maternal instinct would automatically kick in and I would see about my children before ever thinking about me!

I paused to reflect on what I now believed to be unrealistic, irresponsible and unreasonable instructions. Then I forced myself to think about how I might respond if indeed there was an unexpected change in cabin pressure.

Although it would not be the most prudent way to conduct myself, I know that my immediate response would be to frantically run around the cabin to help my travel companions. Just picture it. My first act would be to grab the masks hovering above the heads of a fidgety toddler and a six-year-old. I would then place the masks over their tiny noses, adjust them for a tight fit and then move on to my husband. I repeat this scene as I assisted every member of my family—my mother, my mother-in-law, my father-in-law, my four nieces and their parents. The logical conclusion to this mad and chaotic scene is that sooner—rather than later—I run out of oxygen, pass out and ultimately, provide help to no one.

Reality check!

Put YOUR mask on first!

Why do you think the Federal Aviation Authority requires that these safety regulations are explained prior to every flight? I believe they know that people in general—women and mothers in particular—are more likely to help others first. While it seems like the right thing to do, such a decision is horribly flawed.

It All Started When I Stopped Using Lotion

If I tried to help my girls before I had equipped myself with the life-saving oxygen, I would deplete my air supply, pass out and be of no help to anyone.

While it is highly unlikely that you have to deal with a "sudden change in cabin pressure" on a regular basis, it is highly probable that you are dealing with numerous demands on a daily basis that are depleting your energy levels and your sense of calm.

What demands take precedence over your self-care? When was the last time you said "No" to a request? What are the consequences of meeting the needs of others, while rarely, if ever, taking **TiME**?

Barbara Jenkins, author of *Wit and Wisdom for Women,* categorizes a typical day in the life of today's professional woman:

> "To fill the gap to meet higher mortgages, pay living expenses, take a vacation and save for college or retirement, women are waking up earlier to fix breakfast, stack dishes in the dishwasher, dress the kids, throw on a business suit, apply quick make-up, kiss the kids good-bye at the daycare center and rush off to a high-tech or big-business career."

She goes on to say:

> "...normal life has become an endless stream of work and more work. Women hurry to the grocery store after work, pick up the kids, drop them off at piano lessons, Brownies, soccer and arrive home in time to fix dinner, wash a load of clothes and help with homework before bedtime."

Whew! And let's not forget the hubby who has that special gleam in his eye!

Karen M. R. Townsend, Ph.D.

As professional women holding jobs outside the home, a number of things are often neglected in an attempt to meet the many roles that our careers demand. For some, it might be housework. For others, home-cooked meals. But for far too many, the one thing that is most neglected by us...is US! Why? Because we fail to take our **TiME**.

The scenario is not much different for stay-at-home moms. While some might naively want to switch places with her per the assumption that it is easy to hang out with kids all day, nothing could be further from the truth. Between chauffeuring children to play dates and lessons of every sort, grocery shopping and running errands, stay-at-home moms rarely stay at home.

As a speaker, trainer and consultant, I have the privilege of working with some of the best and brightest women in the country. These women come from a variety of backgrounds and represent a myriad of professions. They are beautiful, intelligent, caring and compassionate. They are leaders in the workplace, volunteers in the community and role models for youth. Who better to provide insight on why we do—or do not—take **TiME**?

I developed a survey to determine how often women take **TiME**. I distributed the *Take Your TiME* assessment to women who attended my workshops, women I met while traveling and even the mothers at my daughters' dance school. These women were demographically diverse—married and single; Baby Boomers to Generation Xers; Black, White, Latina, Asian and Multi-racial; high school graduates to Ph.D.s; stay-at-home moms and career women—yet they shared a common fact.

Before I divulge the "scientific findings" of my extensive survey, I invite you to take a moment to complete the assessment on the following page.

It All Started When I Stopped Using Lotion

Take Your TiME: A Self-Assessment

1. If you had **one day** with no obligations, what would you do?

   _____
   _____
   _____

2. If you had **one hour** just for you, what would you do?

   _____
   _____
   _____

3. In the last **thirty days**, how many times have you done something just for you?

   _____
   _____
   _____

4. What did you do?

   _____
   _____
   _____

5. What prevents you from taking more **TiME**?

   _____
   _____
   _____

The responses to question #5 were quite varied and intriguing. Reasons cited for not taking **TiME** included work obligations, parental responsibilities, pursuing another degree, managing a political campaign, starting a business, attending board meetings, volunteering in the community, etc.

While these responses were echoed by a number of the survey participants, the most common reason for not taking **TiME**—a response shared by sixty-one percent of the women—was because they were "caring for others." These others included children, spouses and significant others, aging parents and in some cases, the family pet.

Of the women who took **TiME**, many of them expressed feeling guilty for doing so. Guilt! Since when is it wrong for me to make Karen a priority? Repeat the question—out loud—substituting my name with yours: Since when is it wrong for **ME** to make (your name here!) a priority?

To borrow from a well-known '70s song performed by R & B artist Luther Ingram, "If loving ME is wrong, I don't want to be right!"

While I do not advocate abandoning your children, neglecting your significant other, limiting the amount of time spent with parents or leaving Rover to fend for himself, I do challenge you to make yourself a priority.

Remember, put your mask on first!

It All Started When I Stopped Using Lotion

How Are You $pending Your TiME?

Perhaps you don't take **TiME** because time is an intangible object that is figuratively and literally impossible to grasp. You can't see it, feel it, taste it, touch it or smell it. You have therefore convinced yourself that time is an elusive, rare commodity.

How often have you wanted to do something for yourself, but then say, "Oh, I'll do it later, when I have more time."? We habitually deny ourselves and then rationalize the decision with excuses like
- I need more time.
- I don't have enough time.
- I have to make more time.

Allow me to be the first to inform you that more time does not exist. We all have the same amount of time each year: 365 days which equates to 8,760 hours. And while we can't make any more, we can become more aware of how we let time slip though our fingers.

Most of us would agree that time is a hard commodity to grasp. Acknowledging that, I invite you to engage in a mental exercise utilizing a commodity with which you are quite familiar: **money!**

Imagine being informed that your wealthy great aunt has just passed away. As her favorite niece, she generously left you $168,000. Exciting, right? Well, Auntie was always a bit eccentric and her penchant for the bizarre did not end with her death. Her attorney informs you that instead of issuing you a check, Auntie left you a bag of cold, hard cash.

Before you can process this monetary blessing or determine how to spend it, your boss informs you that you owe her $40,000. You have no idea as to how she came to that conclusion and before you can object, she reaches into the bag and takes it.

Your husband, kids and other family members decide that they need at least $42,000. Because you love them dearly—and believe that this disbursement is the right thing to do—you oblige the request. They fight and bicker over how to divide the money, so they keep coming back for more. After a while, you lose track of just how much you have given them and they definitely don't know.

Then your church, the non-profit community board on which you sit, your sorority and the Eastern Stars put in bids for contributions. The guilt would consume you like an abyss of darkness, if you didn't share some of your newfound wealth with them. So you allocate $6,000 to the church and $1,000 to each of the other beneficiaries.

Just when you think you have all the bases covered, the tax man calls. He informs you that the IRS demands a minimum of $56,000 and yet another chunk of your money disappears. Based on your best calculations, you have about $11,000 left and you haven't spent one thin dime on yourself.

From $168,000 to $11,000. It just isn't fair! Why should others get more of your money than you?

It All Started When I Stopped Using Lotion

The $168,000 in this fictional account represents the 168 hours that we each have in a week. If we think that it's unfair for others to spend more of our money than we do, isn't it just as unfair for others to $pend more of our **TiME** than we do? Ask yourself this question: How do you $pend—or allow others to $pend—your **TiME**?

Here is the breakdown of how my **TiME** is $pent during an average week. See how it compares to yours.

1. If I'm lucky, I only work forty hours. But more often than not, Lady Luck eludes me and I work considerably more hours.
2. I spend an average of six hours daily—forty-two hours weekly—caring for my family. The morning routine; the evening routine, cooking meals, preparing clothes, helping with homework, etc.
3. My family requires additional time that isn't so predictable. Taxi service to Girl Scouts, play dates, dance practice and shopping for the unexpected birthday party or supplies for the science project. This ex$pense can easily be ten additional hours.
4. Church. I am Baptist. Admittedly, we spend more time in church than some denominations. Add to that committee meetings, choir rehearsals, etc. for about six hours each week.
5. I participate in community groups and attend other meetings as a responsibility of my membership. Add three hours per week to the debit side of my **TiME**.
6. And the IRS request for $56,000 represents the eight hours per night (fifty-six hours per week) of sleep that we are *supposed* to get, but seldom do.

> Note: Too many of us function during waking hours in a sleepy state. This routine is not safe, especially while driving.
>
> According to a 2010 survey released by the AAA Foundation for Traffic Safety, 41% of the 2,000 respondents admitted that at least once, they had fallen asleep or nodded off while driving. Approximately 11% admitted to doing so within the past year and 4% in the previous month. While much emphasis is placed on driving while drunk, studies such as this indicate that sleepy drivers may be just as, if not more, dangerous as drunk drivers.
>
> (Internet Article *Can Driving Drowsy Be Just As Dangerous As Driving Drunk?* by David Sedgwick | AOL Autos; November 23, 2010)

Are you guilty of DWS: Driving While Sleepy?

When I added the time I $pend fulfilling weekly obligations, I had a grand total of 157 hours which left a whopping eleven hours per week for **ME!** More than the shocking revelation of sparse **TiME,** was the tragic realization that I didn't even stake my claim to ownership of the remaining eleven hours. As a result, my life was out of balance.

What about you? How do you $pend your **TiME**?

Use the chart on the next page to assess your **TiME** management for one day—a mere twenty-four hours. Or if you dare, 168 hours—an entire week. You might be surprised by what you discover.

It All Started When I Stopped Using Lotion

How Do You $pend Your TiME?

Indicate the amount of time you
$pend on the following activities:

Working	
Driving / Commuting	
Studying / Helping w/homework	
Preparing meals	
Eating meals	
Exercising	
Watching television	
Working on the computer	
Playing on the computer	
Household chores	
Talking on the phone	
Quality time with family members	
Private time with significant other	
Caring for others	
Self-care	
Sleeping	
Other	
Other	
Total*	

*

Assessment Period	Total Units of Time
Day	24 hours
Week	168 hours

The first time I completed this exercise I realized that I need a thirty-two-hour day! Unfortunately, that just ain't gonna happen!

Ah, but there is good news. While it may appear that you don't have enough **TiME,** today is the day you can renew your commitment to yourself. Lao Tzu said that the journey of a thousand miles begins with one step. The journey from chaos to calm requires only seven steps. Let's take the first step now!

It All Started When I Stopped Using Lotion

Seven Steps
for
Restoring Balance to Your Life

Karen M. R. Townsend, Ph.D.

It All Started When I Stopped Using Lotion

Step One: Do Not Disturb

Okay, I admit it. I stole it.

~ ~ ~ ~

Throughout my career, I have held positions which required me to travel periodically. On one trip, I decided to take a souvenir from my hotel room. While the luxurious towels prove tempting to many travelers and fluffy bathrobes call our names, I wanted the plastic door hanger that slips over the knob when you don't want to be bothered. You know, the one that reads "Do Not Disturb".

I broke the eighth commandment—*Thou shall not steal*—and brought that sign home! I yielded to temptation and stole it for two reasons:

1. I thought about all those times in my life, when I need a moment—or an hour—to myself to wind down and re-energize. I have been known to say to my children, "Unless someone is vomiting, choking, bleeding or unconscious, do not come in my room!" Usually when I get to this point, I am not saying it. I have more than likely reached the place of I-am-at-the-end-of-my-rope and you-have-gotten-on-my-very-last-nerve. By now, I am probably yelling. So when I saw this particular Do Not Disturb sign, I thought that rather than yelling, I mean, telling my children and/or husband that I needed a time-out, the Do Not Disturb sign would be a visual cue to alert them of that fact.

2. This sign was not your typical Do Not Disturb sign. In addition to the directive to stay clear, it had an image of a beautiful woman who appeared to be in her mid-forties. I assumed that she was a corporate type because her attire was professional and impeccable. The most compelling detail—which ultimately lead to the theft—was that this beautiful, impeccably dressed, fortyish, business woman was jumping on the bed. To her credit, she had removed her shoes. A true class act!

I laughed when I imagined corporate executives, traveling saleswomen, motivational speakers, trainers and consultants ending high-powered days of presentations and negotiations by jumping on the beds of this business–class hotel. What a concept!

As I held that Do Not Disturb—soon to be Take Your **TiME**—sign in my hand, I realized that all women probably need one. Not only when traveling for business, but also for day-to-day living. When I am away from home, I have the luxury of informing everyone that I want to be left alone. No guilt or shame is associated with me taking a moment to be completely self-absorbed and self-indulgent. I have never experienced hotel staff incessantly knocking on my door asking what I am doing. I have yet to have a housekeeper stand outside the bathroom and ask when I am coming out.

But in my home...well, that's a different story.

Far be it from me to blame my frenzied home life on the people with whom I live. Dr. Phil said, "We teach people how to treat us." Guilty as charged. I allowed my children to have free reign of my bedroom and come in and out as they pleased. I carried on conversations with a toddler through the bathroom door as I sat on the toilet. I probably should be embarrassed to admit this, but I know that I am not alone. A girlfriend shared with me that once, as she sat on the toilet

It All Started When I Stopped Using Lotion

slow to respond to her toddler's demands, she noticed tiny toddler fingers wiggling under the door. My toddler is now a teenager and she still wants to talk to me while I sit on my throne. She doesn't understand the frustration in my voice or why I command in a stern tone, "Step away from the door!" She just doesn't get that sometimes a woman just wants to poop in peace.

And then, the man who made me a mother—my husband, Sylvester. God bless him! I love that man and after more than two decades together, our relationship has evolved such that we are in harmony on most things. But when it comes to relaxing, our ideas are often diametrically opposed. Down time for me is a bubble bath, fuzzy pajamas and a good book. Down time for him is sitting on the couch in our bedroom—or better yet, lying in the bed—watching ESPN. While my dear husband views being in close proximity as couple time, the experience is quite different for me. I am still trying to master techniques that allow me to max and relax in the bathtub, when right outside the door a grown man is yelling, "Go, Chiefs!"

I needed that sign, so… I stole it. But rather than motivate you to a life of crime, ask yourself, "How can I set boundaries in my home that allow me to renew, refresh and re-energize?"

You can't check into a hotel every time you need to break from your normal routine, but you can establish a do-not-disturb zone in your home.

Start by **honoring yourself**. I shared my evening ritual that had me so focused on the needs of my family that I didn't sit down until 9:30 PM. Well, I challenge you to honor yourself by taking a fifteen-minute retreat every afternoon. This advice was given to me by my therapist, Loretta Murphy

Ms. Murphy suggested that after I walk through the door and greet my children, I should say, "Mommy is going to be in her room for fifteen minutes and then I will come out to hear all about your day."

Now, you try it. Make your announcement and then go directly to your room. Do not pass "Go", do not collect $200 and under no circumstances do you make a detour to start a load of laundry. Go directly to your room!

Once you arrive, honor yourself. For you, honoring yourself, may mean lying on your bed and resting. If you have mastered the art of power napping, fifteen minutes is just enough time to do so. You may use your time to meditate or pray, read a magazine article, remove your makeup, change into comfortable clothes, practice yoga or do Pilates. The choice is yours. What matters most is not what you do, but that you do something just for YOU!

You may be saying, "It's impossible for me to take fifteen minutes. My children need me and they will come looking for me."

I agree. Your children do need you. And you're right. They will come looking for you because "we teach people how to treat us." So why not teach some new lessons?

The first time you attempt to take your fifteen-minute retreat, expect resistance. Your children will not understand your need for **TiME**. If they come looking for you—and they probably will—talk to them in a language they can understand. If you have little ones, tell them that Mommy is taking a time out. Tell older children that you need to chill out. And for your husband....

Okay, let's see. Message to teens: chill out. Message to younger children: time out. What to say to the husband? I imagine a stressed-out mother reading this book and saying, "Can't I just tell him to get out?" I guess you could, but for

It All Started When I Stopped Using Lotion

this strategy to have long-term success, you want your husband or significant other to support your self-care endeavors. Telling him to get out may come across as harsh and may stifle his cooperation. Take a few moments to create a kinder, gentler way of informing him that you need fifteen minutes to renew, refresh and re-energize.

To maximize the probability of having your full fifteen minutes, make advanced provisions for your children. Stock the pantry and fridge with after-school snacks that they can prepare without adult supervision. Designate a place—complete with supplies—that they can use to do homework. And if you are a really bad mom—like me—bend the rules about television and allow them to be couch potatoes while you take your **TiME**.

If you are single or without children, please forgive the frazzled, working moms. We want to believe that it is easier for you to have your afternoon retreat. The assumption is that since you aren't married and/or don't have children, nothing prevents you from taking your **TiME**. We working moms forget that before the husband and children, we had responsibilities that took precedence over our **TiME**.

My friends—those with and without children—struggle to maintain balance in their lives. Beyond the what-do-I-do-with-the-children dilemma, figuring out how to handle the distraction factor is prevalent.

A woman walks into her home after a long day at work, and while she wants to retreat, she is distracted by the laundry that has yet to be folded and put away. So instead of retreating, she folds the clothes. Just as she finishes this task, the phone rings. A telemarketer, who doesn't pause to breathe, pitches the latest deal. After convincing the nuisance that she is not interested in purchasing a time-share in Gatlinburg, a water softener or a free thirty-day membership to the local health club, she hangs up the phone. After a momentary memory lapse, she snaps her fingers. Oh, yeah. The fifteen-minute retreat!

Perhaps it's not the diversion of laundry or other household responsibilities. Perhaps you have a feature on your phone that filters calls from telemarketers. Maybe you don't have typical distractions, but you have 21st-century issues that demand your time and make retreating a challenge.

Many women are part of the sandwich generation: raising children *and* caring for aging parents. The latter responsibility often falls to unmarried women because married siblings have to care for their families. The unspoken expectation: a single woman is available to assume responsibility for the parent who needs extra care. It's logical to assume that a single woman can take on more work, right? Wrong!

Whether married or single; a lactating mother, an empty-nester or childless by choice, you owe it to yourself to take fifteen minutes for yourself—everyday.

Honor yourself with the gift of **TiME**! Why? Because you are worth it. And the byproduct of a happier, healthier you is a more peaceful home.

As the Tina Devaron song, *If Mama Ain't Happy, Ain't Nobody Happy,* so aptly proclaims, we women must be proactive in taking responsibility for the state of our happiness and our sense of peace. So keep this is mind: The next time you need a moment—or an hour—to "get happy" and re-energize, don't yell, scream or kick the cat. Simply excuse yourself, retreat to your room, place your "Do Not Disturb" sign on your door and…jump on the bed!

It All Started When I Stopped Using Lotion

Note: I refuse to assume responsibility for an increase in hotel rates because Do Not Disturb signs are disappearing across the nation. Visit AboutMySisters.com to order your very own Take Your **TiME** door hanger. Remember: *Thou shall not steal!*

Karen M. R. Townsend, Ph.D.

Step Two: Joy!

Ever since I decided to write this book, my dream—like hundreds, maybe even thousands of authors—has been to promote my book on *The Oprah Show*. In trying to develop a plan, gimmick or entree into Oprah's world, I created a scenario as the first step on my journey to her couch.

A regular feature in the magazine is a commentary—usually written by a well-known celebrity—entitled *My Aha! Moment*. One month, the topic was "Joy" with a question about when you had experienced joy. I got the bright idea that if I wrote a great article on joy and submitted it to the magazine, Gayle King—best-friend-in-chief, I mean, the magazine's editor-at-large—would read it and then share it with Oprah. After reading the article, Oprah would instruct her staff to contact me post haste! During the phone conversation, I would casually mention my book and before I knew it, I would be on an American Airlines flight to Chicago!

Seated next to Oprah, I would talk about the premise of the book, explain how my journey from chaos to calm inspired me to share what I had learned with other women and by the end of the show's airing, my book would be on the *New York Times* Bestsellers List. The next day, a Hollywood producer would buy the movie rights and soon thereafter, I would retire to Paradise Island in the Bahamas! Yes, that was the plan!

To set the overnight-success strategy in motion, I had to first write an article about what brings me joy.

Okay, easy enough. I sat at the desk in my home office, grabbed a pen and paper and then prepared to capture the flood of joyful memories.

The thing that brings me joy is...

I tapped my pen on the arm of the chair. My mind was blank, so I rephrased the statement.

I experience joy when...

My mind was still blank.

The last time I experienced joy in my life was...

Nothing. Nothing. Nothing!

I started to believe that I had no joy in my life. I could not come up with one, single, solitary example of joy.

Just as I leaned forward and cupped my head in my hands, my then two-year-old daughter, KaeLyn, toddled into the room. She came to where I was seated, pulled papers off the desk, threw the pencils and pens on the floor and then scurried away. The disturbance momentarily broke my train of thought. As I bent to pick up the mess, KaeLyn returned. This time she wanted a kiss. I kissed her, patted her bottom and then sent her own her way. Moments later, she returned. Although she couldn't talk well, she made it clear that she wanted a hug. So I hugged her.

This game continued for about ten minutes and made it increasingly more difficult for me to concentrate on what brought me joy. When KaeLyn came over for what seemed the millionth time, I almost exploded. But then it struck me. This sweet little angel, who had a few teeth, very little hair and limited communication skills, brought me joy! She loved me unconditionally and all she asked for in return were tight hugs and wet kisses. I experienced an aha moment in the form of a diaper-clad, pacifier-sucking, office-destroying

It All Started When I Stopped Using Lotion

toddler. KaeLyn was a living, breathing, real-life example of joy in my life.

I reflected on the day that KaeLyn was born and remembered that my husband and I cried tears of joy. My sister-in-law was also present for the birth. Although Sonya is the mother of four children, she had never witnessed a baby's birth. Sonya stood near the bed, rubbed my head, prayed with me and experienced her own joy when KaeLyn made her entrance into the world.

My friend, Jacquie, was there, too. Her job was to videotape the birth. I often tease her that she should give up her government job to become a professional videographer. Her color commentary and play-by-play voiceovers documented the joyous occasion. Before KaeLyn was born, Jacquie explained to her how much she was loved and how anxious we all were to meet her. That, my friends, was joy!

My daughter, Syron, who was four-and-a-half at the time, was also anxious for her sister to "come out." She waited at Aunt Sonya's house—yet again—for her sister to be born. She was aware that Mommy had gone to the hospital two other times and came home without a baby. So, December 5, 1998 represented joy for her because Sissy was finally here!

As I sat at my desk massaging my temples, I could not think of one example of joy. But when I took **TiME** to look around, I found myself in the midst of joy. I was just too close to recognize it.

H. Jackson Browne, Jr. summed it up perfectly in his 1993 work, *Life's Little Instruction Book*: "Don't overlook life's small joys while seeking the big ones."

By the way, every time I speak my daughters' names, I relive a joyful experience. Syron—which has its origin in the West African Yoruba language—means joy. KaeLyn is Gaelic and means rejoice. I often tell the girls that with my first daughter I had *joy* and with my second daughter I *rejoiced.* Joy to the world!

The Merriam-Webster Dictionary defines joy as "a source or cause of delight; a state of happiness; the emotion evoked by well-being, success, good fortune or by the prospect of possessing what one desires."

Ponder this question:

How do you define joy? More importantly—what brings you joy?

As you journey from chaos to calm, identify those things that bring you joy. While some joy is dependent upon the involvement of others (i.e. receiving hugs and kisses from those we love), you also need to identify those things that bring you joy on a purely personal and individual level.

In a 2008 survey conducted by MomLogic.com, 700 busy, stay-at-home and working moms were asked what made them most happy. Can you guess the top response? *Time.* And not just more time to do something with or for someone else. These women indicated that they desired to have more **TiME** alone. Time for ME!

Women after my own heart. Courageous enough to embrace—and articulate—that they need, crave and desire **TiME**. Many of them specified what they wanted to do with the **TiME**: spend it in the bathtub! Obviously, I am not the only busy, working woman with an under-utilized Jacuzzi!

Other survey responses included
- Working out
- Taking a family vacation
- Getting a massage
- A romantic date with a spouse or significant other
- Playing with kids/husband
- Doing nothing
- Sleeping

It All Started When I Stopped Using Lotion

Note: These findings were submitted by MomLogic.com and reported in *Today's Christian Woman*, July/August 2009 issue.

Now it's your turn. Think about what makes you happy or brings you joy. What are some of your favorite things to do? Because I don't want these things to slip your mind, write your responses on the next page.

Karen M. R. Townsend, Ph.D.

These are a few of my favorite things...

Oscar Hammerstein II
The Sound of Music

In the space below, list some of the favorite things you LOVE to do. Include things that you do on a regular basis, as well as, things you may not have done in a while.

These should be ME things that make YOU happy and bring you JOY.

_____

_____

_____

_____

_____

_____

_____

_____

_____

_____

It All Started When I Stopped Using Lotion

Questions to consider:

1. How many items did you list?
   _____
   _____
   _____

2. Was it easy or difficult for you to create your list? Why or why not?
   _____
   _____
   _____

3. Are all the items listed ME things or did you include activities that are in service to others?
   _____
   _____
   _____

4. If you included activities in service to others, how do they compare with the number of items you included in service to self?
   _____
   _____
   _____

   a. What, if anything, does this mean to you?
   _____
   _____
   _____

5. Review your list. How many of these favorite things have you done in the last thirty days? The last sixty days?

_____

_____

_____

6. If you have favorite things that you have not done in the last sixty days, what has prevented you from doing so?

_____

_____

_____

It All Started When I Stopped Using Lotion

Whenever I include this activity in workshops and retreats, an overwhelming number of women admit that they are *not* doing their favorite things. I used to think that money was the issue, but after listening to the women, it became clear. The reason women are not engaging in their favorite things is not a lack of money. More often than not, women are not engaging in their favorite things because of a lack of **TiME!**

Oh yes! I love to lie on the beach at the Atlantis Resort on Paradise Island in the Bahamas, but I also love to take bubble baths in my Jacuzzi. The former costs big money. The latter costs a little **TiME.**

I challenge you to take another look at your list of favorite things and then commit to do at least one thing this week. Next week, do another thing and the following week, another; and the following week, another....My hope is that you will do at least one thing that brings you joy *every day!*

As I mentioned in a previous chapter, I used to think that my life would be much easier if I had days that were thirty-two hours long. Then I realized that all I would probably do is fill those eight extra hours with more work. I now understand that to restore and maintain balance, we must make a conscious effort to do so every day. Of course there will be times when we will be consumed by the responsibilities of our professions. Or days when our families will demand our full and complete attention. But if we continue catering to the needs and demands of others, and never take the time to do those things that are special and important to us—the things that bring us JOY!—we will be the ones who suffer the most.

Barbara Jenkins in *Wit and Wisdom for Women* said that it is important for women to take time to relax, read, laugh and have fun.

These things don't happen on their own. You have to plan for them and then take the **TiME** to do them. In my experience, I have learned that all work and no play makes a woman…mean!

Identify those things that bring you JOY. Then as that classic Nike slogan so appropriately states, "Just do it!"

It All Started When I Stopped Using Lotion

Step Three: Build a Chaos to Calm Team

How many times have you heard someone say, "Diets don't work"?

If you have ever been up watching television late at night or in the wee hours of the morning, then you have probably seen a weight-loss infomercial and heard that statement.

You may be asking, "What in the world does dieting have to do with moving from chaos to calm?"

Excellent question! Many diets don't work because most of them are temporary fixes. Anyone can eat cabbage soup, drink meal-replacement shakes or consume large quantities of cayenne pepper and maple syrup lemonade for a short period of time, but such a diet will fail over time. Healthcare professionals, dieticians, nutritionists and personal trainers all agree that permanent weight loss requires daily commitment to a lifestyle change.

Let's say that you find the perfect dress and decide to buy it one size smaller as an incentive to lose ten pounds. You might squeeze into the dress for a wedding, class reunion or Christmas party, but will it still fit in three months? Doubt it! Unless you have made a lifestyle change, the chances are slim to none that it will.

People who lose weight and keep it off attribute the success to lifestyle changes and support systems. Weight Watchers, Curves and similar programs promote not only exercising and sensible eating, but lifestyle changes and group support.

When you decide to lose weight, more than likely you will face many temptations. Unless you have a team of people who support your healthy goals, the probability that you'll fall off the wagon is extremely high.

Dedication is required to move from a frenzied, chaotic life to one of peace, harmony and calm. As you attempt to make a commitment to take your **TiME**, make yourself a priority and incorporate self-care into your weekly—and hopefully, daily—routine, you'll need a network of supporters. Who will be on your Chaos to Calm (CTC) Team?

You may start as a team of one, but be not discouraged. If you struggle to find women who are ready to make themselves a priority, once they see the positive change in you, they will want to join your program.

In the meantime, the following ideas will support your lifestyle commitment:

1. **Have a clear understanding as to why you are making this change**. If your doctor informed you that you had high blood pressure and heart disease, you would take better care of your body to avoid premature death. Well, I am a doctor (**Dr.** Karen M.R. Townsend) and as such I feel compelled to assess the current state of your health. Since I haven't seen you in my office and I am *not* a medical doctor, I will rely on my psychic, I mean, intuitive powers to access your chaos-to-calm quotient. I have a hunch that at some point in your life—probably on more than one occasion—you have been referred to as a Superwoman. I would also wager that you spend much of your time in service to others. Considering all those factors, are you ready and willing to make the change? If so, explain why. Because a big enough *why*

will compel you to come up with the *how*. WHY do you want to make a lifestyle change?

_____

_____

_____

_____

2. **Define what self-care means to you.** For me, self-care means making ME a priority. Getting enough sleep, honoring my body with healthy and nutritious foods, exercising regularly, spending time with loved ones. What does self-care mean to you? More importantly, what does self-care look like in YOUR life?

_____

_____

_____

_____

3. **Make a commitment to care for yourself.** Take another look at how you defined self-care. Now, take out your calendar, planner, Blackberry, Palm Pilot—or whatever device you use to schedule your time—and make a date with yourself to do one of the self-care activities you identified. I realize that it is virtually impossible to prioritize your schedule, so instead, schedule your priorities. Starting today, YOU are the priority.

My self-care activity is:

_____

_____

_____

I commit to engage in this activity by this date:

_____

4. **Warning: Not everyone will understand or support your decision to make YOU a priority.** Run away from them! Although the changes suggested thus far are quite positive, expect to be met with a few negative reactions. Some will be unable to grasp your new outlook on life, especially if the way you used to live your life—frenzied and chaotic—is the way they still choose to live theirs. As a result, rather than applaud your progressive choices, they may question your actions and motives as follows:

"Why are you missing the meeting to get a massage?"

"Do you really have to go to the spa today?"

"I can't believe you are actually going to spend the whole day in bed!"

In the event that you are faced with any of the above-listed hypothetical comments, I have provided some possible responses:

"Why are you missing the meeting to get a massage?"

"Duh! Because I can!"

"Do you really have to go to the spa today?"

"No, I don't have to. I choose to!"

"I can't believe you are actually going to spend the whole day in bed!"

"Believe it!"

5. **When you make YOU a priority, you will be better equipped to have a positive effect on others.** Conversely, when you care for yourself poorly, all areas of your life suffer. Be your best so that you can do your best and give your best. When you think of it in those terms, your self-care becomes a win-win for everyone in your life.

6. **Invite others to join your quest for self-care.** After a few weeks of self-care, I predict that your whole attitude about life and the way you live it will change. And people will notice. When they inquire, be honest and say, "I've changed! I am now the priority in my life." Share how you are living your life for the better and encourage them to join you. In doing so, you will create your CTC Team—one recovering Superwoman at a time! Think about who would be great members on your CTC Team. Write the names of the top draft picks for your team in the space below. Contact them this week with an invitation to join you on this journey.

_____

_____

_____

_____

7. **Resources are important as you build your CTC Team.** In addition to using this book on your own journey from chaos to calm, I have a list of books that have been extremely helpful to me. In the early days

of my journey, when I did not have anyone to talk to about how I felt, these authors offered me the encouragement I needed to stay the course. Not everyone understood or respected my commitment to self-care. Without the support and reinforcement from these self-care Superwomen, I would not have completed my journey.

- *Patches of Inspiration* by Sonie Bigbee
- *Uncommon Sense: For Real Women in the Real World* by Suzette Brawner and Jill Brawner Jones
- *I'm Here, Now What? A Woman's Guide In Corporate America* by Toni Perry Gillispie
- *Sacred Pampering Principles* by Debrena Jackson Gandy
- *Wit and Wisdom for Women* by Barbara Jenkins
- *KeyNotes* by Stacey Lawson
- *The Frazzled Female: 30 Days to Finding God's Peace In Your Daily Chaos* by Cindy Wood

While you scout local members for your CTC Team, consider adding these ladies and their books to your virtual team.

Since this chapter has been about building a team, it seems only fitting that I include cheerleaders. Because I was a cheerleader in high school, I understand the importance of encouraging the team, especially at the beginning of the season.

It All Started When I Stopped Using Lotion

As you begin what may be a new season of self-care—even if you are a team of one—I offer you this cheer:

It's time to get started.
It's time to begin.
YOU are worthy of self-care;
Commit to it and win!
Gather your girlfriends;
Create your team.
Find balance together;
It's not just a dream.
I'm number one!
The priority is ME!
If you value self-care,
Join Team CTC!

Karen M. R. Townsend, Ph.D.

It All Started When I Stopped Using Lotion

Step Four: Just Say, "No!"

In the long run, even though it might be a hard thing to do, it is better to say "No" in the beginning than to say "Yes" and fail to live up to your commitments.

Suzettee Brawner & Jill Brawner Jones
Uncommon Sense: For Real Women in the Real World

In the 1980s, *"Just Say No!"* was used by then First Lady Nancy Reagan as a battle cry against drug usage. The children of that era—including me—were taught to respond to offers of drugs by just saying, "No!"

Some twenty-plus years later, I am proud to say that I made it through the '80s, '90s and the first decade of the new millennium without becoming addicted to drugs. Unfortunately, I have to confess to another type of addiction: always saying "Yes." I have heard some refer to this malady as "the disease to please." Call it what you will—a disease, a disorder, an illness or a syndrome—scores of women suffer from this ailment. And just like any other addiction, you think you have control over it, when it really controls you.

Think for a moment. How many times this week have you said "Yes" and then afterward, regretted your decision? You may have even asked yourself, "Why did I agree to yet another commitment?"

Why? Because you couldn't help yourself.

You are addicted to saying, "Yes."

Don't get me wrong—I am not pointing the finger at you. Because like the saying goes, "Whenever you point your finger at someone, three fingers point back at you." So true. You see, I, too, am addicted to saying "Yes." And my saga played out in the not so distant past.

It was the beginning of the school year, and as always, an open house had been planned so that parents, students and teachers could meet and connect. Because I had always volunteered in the past, the president of the Parent Teacher Organization called to ask if I could bring treats for the open house. Simple request, right? Wrong!

While I immensely enjoy helping at both my daughters' schools, this particular open house fell at an extremely busy time for me. I had just returned from an out-of-state, multiple-day training and I was in the final stages of creating a five-day leadership development program. Not to mention all the other beginning-of-the-school-year activities: permission slips, medical documents, field-trip release forms, school supplies, school clothes and more. With all these things in mind, the intelligent response, the logical response, the simple response to this request was "No." But guess what. I said, "Yes."

Why in the world—knowing that I was already overscheduled, overbooked and on the verge of being overwhelmed—would I ever agree to bring treats to the open house? And not just any treat. No, I committed to bringing Krispy Kreme Donuts: a confectionary delicacy. Oh, and did I mention that the only Krispy Kreme Donut shop in my city is about thirty minutes from my house? Do the math: a sixty-minute round trip...for donuts!

Why in the world did I agree to bring donuts to a middle-school open house? In my heart, I wanted to decline the

It All Started When I Stopped Using Lotion

request, but somewhere between my heart, my brain and my mouth, I accepted. Why? Because I wanted to be perceived as the involved parent. I wanted the ladies who ran the parents' group to say, "Even with all that she has to do, you can always depend on Dr. Townsend." I said "Yes" when I should have said "No" because I was out of control! Looking back on this whole situation, I have asked myself over and over again, "What were you thinking?" That's just it. I wasn't thinking. I couldn't think because my addiction had taken over.

But wait, there's more. I agreed to bring the Krispy Kreme Donuts and then forgot that I had made the commitment, until one hour before the event! Now remember, the round trip from my house to the donut shop is sixty minutes, plus an additional twenty-minute drive to the school which is in the opposite direction! Believe it or not, I actually contemplated how I could get from one end of the county to the other in less than sixty minutes!

When I finally came to my senses, I devised a new plan: take one of my lovely glass, I mean *crystal* platters, stop by the superstore which is en route to the middle school, purchase cookies, place them on the platter and attempt to pass them off as homemade. That was the plan.

Although my husband and I were supposed to ride together, I had to leave early to purchase my "homemade" cookies. He would just have to meet me at school.

Runners, take you mark. Ready…Set…Go! The race was on.

I sprinted to my car, sped to the store, parked as close as possible to the entrance and then dashed inside. I was pleasantly surprised to see a table of "homemade" sugar cookies prominently displayed near the front door. This was proof that fairy godmothers do exist! I exhaled, grabbed the cookies, checked myself out at the first available U-Scan aisle and then ran back to my car.

With the car idling, I took the cookies out of the plastic container and then lovingly placed them on the glass, I mean, *crystal* platter. The mere act of transferring the cookies from plastic to platter magically transformed them into homemade cookies. I covered my cookies with plastic wrap and then sped to the open house.

When I arrived at the school, I went directly to the cafeteria to drop-off the treats. Imagine my surprise when I saw table upon table of treats. Some of which I am sure were *actually* homemade.

In that moment, I realized that in this case "No" really would have been an appropriate response. With so many sweets, my treats would not even have been missed. But instead, I promised to do something that I didn't want to do, and in the attempt to be a woman of my word, I almost went nuts! Nuts over a commitment to bring donuts!

Since that time, donuts have become symbolic for me. When I reflect back on that incident, I realize that in my quest to provide donuts, I almost went nuts! The metaphor is this: When you **DO** too much, you run the risk of going *NUTS*! So the next time you contemplate accepting a request without fully thinking the matter through, consider this: Are you about to do a "donut?"

So how do we (this includes me) get over our addiction to saying "Yes"? What is the solution? Do we need to go to *Yes Sayers Anonymous*? Do we need a twenty-eight-day stint in rehab to participate in group-therapy sessions to freely and openly discuss our options before we make decisions? What to do? What to do?

Since I have not yet located a chapter of *Yes Sayers Anonymous* in my community—and I can't take time out of

It All Started When I Stopped Using Lotion

my life to go to rehab for twenty-eight days—I have developed a treatment plan: *KT's 10-Step Decision-Making Process.*

Let me clarify. The purpose of KT's Ten-Step Decision Making Process is not to provide an excuse, rationale or road map to saying "No." Rather, it serves as a formula or guide to critically assess whether you should say "Yes."

Let's be honest. Think about the last request someone made of your time, money, involvement or expertise. Did you thoroughly consider the request or did you respond automatically? For me, in far too many cases, the latter reigned supreme. I wish I could say that I took a *little* time to consider the requests people made of my **TiME**. However, in most cases, I took *no* time. In so doing, I said "Yes," when in many cases, I should have said "No."

Before you can resolve a problem, you must admit that you have one. Well, here it goes: My name is Karen Marie Reynolds Townsend and I am a yes-aholic.

I want to go on the record and say that it is not my intention to make light of any person who is battling an addiction. But rather to emphasize that too many women are saying "yes" too often. These increased commitments, responsibilities and obligations lead to increased stress.

Studies conducted by medical and mental-health professionals revealed that now more than ever, the health of American women is dramatically affected by stress. Although you might not recognize it—or be willing to admit it—the hustle and bustle of life in the 21st century has taken a toll on our health. As you attempt to juggle the demands of family, work, finances and the like, stress presents itself in the form of headaches, irritability, insomnia, fatigue, weight gain and chest pain. Over time, this "yes" addiction will have the same results as years of smoking, drinking and drug abuse: diminished health and shortened life.

I don't want this fate to be yours, so I offer you KT's 10-Step Decision-Making Process:

Step 1: What was your gut reaction? Regardless of who made the request (spouse, parent, sibling, child, co-worker, boss, spiritual leader, neighbor, friend, etc.), what was your immediate physical reaction? Did your body respond with excitement and anticipation or did you mask your true feelings?

Step 2: How much time must you invest? Remember, you only have 168 hours per week to invest in all of your personal, professional, social, spiritual and emotional endeavors. Is this activity where you want to $pend your **TiME**?

Step 3: How much money must you invest? In addition to the time element, many of the commitments we are asked to consider require an investment of financial resources. Before you respond to any request, find out how much money it is going to ¢o$t you.

Step 4: How will this decision affect your family? On the surface, it might not seem as though this request has anything to do with your family; however, consider how saying "Yes" will infringe upon the already limited time with your spouse—or significant other—and if you have any, your children. Heck, you may even need to consider how this decision affects your pets: If you are away, who is going to walk Fido?

Step 5: How will this decision affect your career goals? It's easy to convince yourself that it's only one more committee or task force or board seat or _____ (you fill in the blank). But is this "only one more" consistent with your career goals? Will this "only one more" give you an opportunity to showcase your skills in front of those who can make a difference in your promotability? Will this "only one more" get you closer to your professional vision?

Step 6: How will this decision affect your relationships with family and friends? Will this decision enhance your family life? Can you share this opportunity with your friends? Will your involvement contribute to or detract from your already limited time with the people that you say are the most important to you?

Step 7: What are the risks and opportunities? Businesses conduct feasibility studies before launching a new venture. They critically analyze how a potential project or prospect could benefit or harm the current state of operations. Take the **TiME** to run your own feasibility study before responding to requests.

Step 8: What are the pros and cons? Just in case you skipped Step 7, I rephrased it. Before you make a decision about this request, carefully assess the possible affect on your already busy life. Take a sheet of paper. Draw a line down the middle to create two columns. Label one column "Pros" and the other "Cons". Use this "Pro and Cons" sheet as a tool to fully contemplate your decision. What is good about this request? How will you benefit from this opportunity? How will others be served by your involvement? Conversely, what is *not so good* about this request? What will you have to give up by being involved? Is this request really an opportunity—or simply another obligation? This simple black-and-white assessment may help you make a much better decision.

Step 9: What will happen if you say, "No?" Go there for a moment. Close your eyes, take a deep breath and then exhale. Now imagine what will happen if you say, "No."

Will the committee cease to function? Will the event be cancelled? Will the project lose funding? Will your daughter *really* die if you don't drive her to the mall to get that new dress, CD or latest and greatest Bratz doll? I doubt it. In some cases your "Yes" will be critical, but in most cases, life will go on.

Step 10: Have you prayed about it? While I have a number of years of professional experience and a total of twenty-three years of formal education (that is, if you count kindergarten), I am astutely aware that I don't have all the answers. In many cases, even after consulting with friends, family members and professional colleagues, I still have to put my all on the altar. If you were raised in a Baptist church, you're familiar with this phrase. I go to God. Not knowing your religious beliefs—or if you even espouse to a belief in a higher power—I want to share something that has played an important part in my life: prayer.

Connection and spirituality for you may come through quiet meditation or a walk in nature. Whatever the strategy, we often gain the courage to make the hard decisions by calling upon a power greater than ourselves.

As I re-read this chapter, I felt good about what I had written. Then my teen-age daughter—the one whose open house almost drove me nuts—declared in her adolescent wisdom, "Mommy, no one is going to use all of those steps before they make a decision. That's not even realistic."

And a little child shall lead them.

I was humbled and she was right.

My realistic expectation is not that you will use every step before you make every decision. However, my genuine hope is that you will pick three, two or even one. By doing so, you will only commit to those things that matter most and thus

It All Started When I Stopped Using Lotion

honor yourself and those around you. And for those things that aren't a priority, you will free yourself to "Just say, No!"

Karen M. R. Townsend, Ph.D.

KT's 10-Step Decision Making Process

The ten steps are repeated here with space for you to write your answers. Use this page when facing complicated decisions or when determining whether to take treats to your children's school.

1. What is my gut reaction?

   _____

2. How much time must I invest?

   _____

3. How much money must I invest?

   _____

4. How will this decision affect my family?

   _____

5. How will this decision affect my career goals?

   _____

6. How will this decision affect my relationship with family and friends?

   _____

7. What are the risks and opportunities?

   _____

8. What are the pros and cons?

   _____

9. What will happen if I say "No"?

   _____

10. Have I prayed about it?

    _____

It All Started When I Stopped Using Lotion

Step Five: Just Say, "Yes!"

Someone once told me that every time we say "Yes" to one request, we are saying "No" to something else. While most of us are quite skilled at saying "Yes" for the benefit of others, we are not so inclined when the "Yes" benefits us. In this chapter, we will focus on how to say "Yes!" to yourself.

~ ~ ~ ~

Have you ever been tempted to run away from home? (Tell the truth. It'll be our secret.) Not only have I been tempted, I did it!

The first time I ran away from home I was six years old. I can't quite remember the circumstances that prompted me to run; however, I do remember the following:
- It was a Sunday afternoon, after church.
- I wore only the slip which had been under my Sunday-go-to-meeting dress.
- I didn't go too far—just across the street.
- I didn't run. I walked.
- I got in big trouble for leaving the house without permission—and for doing so while only wearing a slip!

That act of defiance occurred over forty years ago and since that initial run, I have been known to leave the house without permission on numerous occasions.

Although I cannot recall the catalyst for my inaugural escape at age six, I know exactly why I ran away from home at thirty-three. I was in desperate need of **TiME**. The challenges of being a wife, mother, employee, entrepreneur, student, volunteer and aunt-sister-girlfriend had overtaken and consumed me. I just needed to get away. The decision wasn't easy for me, especially when I recalled a conversation that I had with a friend and her husband a few years prior.

Charlene and I have known each other for over twenty-five years. We first met as newly hired recruiters for The Ohio State University. We worked together Monday through Friday, traveled together and shared hotel rooms from August to December during recruitment season. We invested so much time together that we became great friends.

Although we no longer work together or even live in the same city, the bond of our friendship remains. I learned the Electric Slide at her wedding and we agreed to be godmothers to each others' first born.

Some years ago, I learned that Charlene and I would be attending the same national conference in San Antonio, Texas. I was so excited that I would get the chance to see her and catch up with everything that was going on in her life. Her husband, John, was also attending which enhanced the opportunity to reconnect.

During our reunion, Charlene and I had a conversation about the challenges of motherhood.

I said, "Sometimes I feel like I just want to run away from home so I can have some peace, quiet and time for myself. If I had just a weekend to myself, I would come back refreshed, renewed and better equipped to meet all the demands of my life."

John didn't seem to understand why I felt the need to flee to relax. He believed that every person should be able to relax in their own home.

It All Started When I Stopped Using Lotion

While I agree that every person *should* be able to relax at home, that has proven to be a difficult task for me. When I talk to other women, many of them say that they struggle with the same dilemma.

Now, don't get me wrong. I am blessed to have a home that is quite comfortable. However, for some reason, the ability to relax often eludes me.

I am amazed by my husband's ability to come home from work and—in the midst of kids, clutter and chaos—totally relax. He comes in the door, kisses me, greets his girls, takes his place on the couch, grabs the remote and for the next several hours, he can totally chill. I am so jealous!

I, on the other hand, can only sit on the couch and watch television without feeling guilty if I have a basket of clothes to fold while watching taped episodes of *The Oprah Show* and *Grey's Anatomy*. (They have been taped because during the original broadcast, I didn't have **TiME** to watch them!) I guess you could say that I view "working while I watch" as a sort of penance. It is my way of earning the right to watch television.

This behavior had become so habitual that my older daughter, Syron, admonished me. As the opening credits rolled on a movie we prepared to watch, I retrieved a basket of laundry.

Syron said, "Mommy, just watch the movie. Don't fold any clothes."

What lessons had I taught my daughters? What habits are you instilling in your daughter? Will your son expect the same work-until-you-drop foolishness from his companion?

The perpetual distractions followed me from room to room—dishes, laundry, bills—and sidetracked my ability to relax. How dare I relax in the midst of the major to-do list also known as my home? I decided that I needed to run away from home.

I first ran away over ten years ago. (Yes, I said first because now I do it on a regular basis.) I disappeared under the guise of going on a business trip. I drove from Dayton to Cincinnati, Ohio and checked in the Omni Netherland Hotel. Because I am so anal about everything, I even made a to-do list for my **TiME** away. Am I sick or what?

I made the list because I wanted to ensure that I did as many of my favorite things as possible. My list included the following:

- Reading the magazines that I subscribe to, but rarely have **TiME** to read.
- Holding the remote in *my* hand and watching what *I* want on television. (If you have a husband or significant other, then you know why this was such a big deal for me!)
- Taking a long, relaxing bubble bath and then slathering my body with lotion.
- Sleeping in the middle of the king-sized bed while wearing my most non-sexy pajamas.
- Sleeping until I woke up. Message: Not because an alarm clock, child or spouse had awakened me.
- Ordering breakfast in bed to enjoy a meal that I didn't cook or have to clean up afterwards.
- Creating a Dream Board. This visual display would include everything I wanted to be, do or have.

Thinking back on that time away calms me. I go back to a time and place when I made myself the priority. My only regret about that first excursion was that I didn't have the courage to tell my husband my true intentions. I knew that if I told him I had a business trip, he would not question my two-day absence. However, I'm not sure what his reaction would have been if I had announced, "Honey, I am about to lose my mind, so to maintain my sanity, I am running away from home!" I didn't give him the opportunity because I was unwilling to tell him my truth.

In the years since, my husband's reaction to my quarterly "disappearing acts" has grown to be quite positive. He is all for it. Sometimes he even foots the bill! One of the blessings of being married to a man for almost half your life is that he comes to know you—the real you. My husband can sense when I need a break. With all the love in his heart, he has been known to say, "Why don't you get away for a couple of days?"

Now, I don't have to run away. I just check into a hotel. Book a trip. Take a cruise. That's right, a cruise. For my fortieth birthday, I took a cruise all by myself! Many people offered to go with me, but when I anticipated the milestone birthday, I thought it would be grand to spend that time with someone with whom I had become disconnected. Someone with whom I felt out of touch. Someone with whom I needed to re-establish a loving and caring relationship. That person was Me!

Yes, Me!

I love that two-word combination—Yes and Me.

The older I get, the more I realize that it is perfectly fine for me to say "Yes" to me. "Yes" to me does not negate my commitment to family. "Yes" to me does not diminish the love I have for my husband or daughters. "Yes" to me by no means indicates that I am unwilling to be of service to my friends, my church or my community.

"Yes" to me means that I have finally realized that if my life is out of balance, my capacity to love, ability to commit and desire to serve will be negatively impacted. My choice, therefore, is to put a positive spin on the challenges of life balance by saying "Yes" to me.

Saying "Yes" to yourself is positive, affirming and most importantly, necessary to move from chaos to calm.

Here is an opportunity for you to practice saying "Yes" to yourself.

- Could you benefit from an hour to yourself? *Answer:* Just say, "Yes!"
- Could you benefit from an afternoon to yourself? *Answer:* Just say, "Yes!"
- Could you benefit from a day to yourself? *Answer:* Just say, "Yes!"
- Could you benefit from a weekend to yourself? *Answer:* Just say, "Yes!"

Now, a more difficult question:

Within the next twenty-four hours, will you take out your calendar, look at your schedule and plan **TiME** for yourself? (No prompting here. It's up to you. Hint: Just say, "Yes!")

Finally, the hardest question of all:

After you make the plan (I have confidence in you), will you put your plan into action and take your **TiME** in the next thirty days?

Just…say…"Yes!"

It All Started When I Stopped Using Lotion

Step Six: PMS - It's Not What You Think!

What three letters can strike fear into the minds of men and elicit the sympathy of any woman who has experienced a visit from her monthly friend? **PMS**.

Most of us have been conditioned to respond negatively when we hear, see or read those three letters in that particular order because we all know what they stand for.

PMS equals Pre-Menstrual Syndrome, right?

Wrong! From this day forward, whenever you see PMS, I want you to resist the automatic response that says pre-menstrual syndrome and replace it with **P**amper **M**y**S**elf!

We all need a little PMS every now and then. And if you aren't proactive about incorporating it into your life regularly (monthly would be great), you may be compelled to do so when things get completely out of control.

~ ~ ~ ~

A while back, I went on a sensory journey. That is what LaVonda, my esthetician called it. I had not planned to take a trip of any sort, let alone a sensory journey, but journey I did.

The impetus for this journey? My reflection in the mirror.

While performing my normal morning routine—washing my face, brushing my teeth, putting on makeup—I took a good look in the mirror. The image looking back startled me: a middle-aged woman with bushy eyebrows, blotchy skin and four whiskers growing out of her chinny chin chin!

My first response was to laugh at the pitiful woman resembling a creature raised by wolves, but when I realized that I was looking at myself, I wanted to cry.

Instead, I called Square One—my spa of choice in Dayton, Ohio—and booked an appointment for a brow wax. Before ending the call, I said, "What the heck! I'll get a facial, too!" Little did I know, I was setting the stage for my sensory journey.

One of the items on my list of "100 Things To Do Before I Die" is to establish a standing monthly spa appointment. It sounds good in theory, but I found it very hard to put into practice on a consistent basis. This lack of consistency had now resulted in the need for an emergency PMS treatment.

My motivation for writing this book was to convince super busy women to take your **TiME**. With that, I must also acknowledge that saying it is far easier than doing it. Whenever I am overtaxed and overwhelmed, it seems as though my commitment to personal hygiene and grooming goes out the window. Don't get me wrong. I still shower and brush my teeth, but anything beyond that is a luxury. And you know how we busy, working women accommodate luxuries. By fitting them in if, and only if, we have **TiME**. Well, if you haven't figured it out by now, the only way we will have **TiME**, is if we are intentional about taking **TiME**.

The phone call to Square One was my cry for help. A desperate plea. The realization and acknowledgement that I was in need of pampering. I decided it was **TiME** for me to indulge in PMS.

The symptoms that lead me to seek a PMS experience were the bushy eyebrows and unwanted facial hair. Imagine Boris Karloff in Universal's *Werewolf* wearing a Jones New York business suit. That was me! If you have noticed that your patience has been running thin in way too many

It All Started When I Stopped Using Lotion

situations, you might need to pursue a PMS experience. Perhaps you have noticed that your tolerance levels are diminishing causing you to become easily agitated and irritated. Perhaps you no longer participate in the things that used to bring you joy and instead find yourself self-medicating to ease your discomfort. Maybe every day someone gets on your very last nerve. Perhaps, like me, your self-care in the area of grooming and hygiene has suffered. I know what it looked like for me and if you are honest with yourself, you can identify what it looks like for you. Once you identify it, the next step is to do something about it. Your challenge may be determining what to do when you know you need to do something. I suggest a sensory journey.

When I arrive at Square One, calmness overtakes me. The natural aroma of Aveda products, the ambiance created by distinctive interior design and the commitment to customer service make Square One my favorite spa retreat. Brent, one of the owners of this establishment, greeted me with his typical upbeat persona. He informed me that my esthetician would be with me shortly.

Moments later, LaVonda appeared and offered me a beverage and then led me to the treatment room. She lit several fragranced candles, dimmed the lights and then said, "Karen, remove your earrings, necklace and clothing from the waist up." LaVonda left the room and gently closed the door to allow for my privacy.

What? I am only having a facial! Why do I have to get half-naked?

My hesitancy to shed my clothes lasted a few short seconds. I decided to go a step further than instructed and I removed my jeans, too. Why not be totally comfortable? I removed my clothing down to my undies, climbed on the table and then covered myself with the softest blanket that had every touched my skin. With flickers of light dancing on the ceiling and tranquil music playing, I awaited LaVonda's return.

When she entered the room, she said, "I'll begin with the eyebrow wax. I don't want to get you totally relaxed and then stress you out by waxing your brows."

Totally relaxed. What a concept. The expectation excited me.

If you have had your eyebrows waxed, then you know that the experience is many things, but relaxing is not one of them. You try to prepare yourself and anticipate the moment the muslin cloth covering the heated wax will rip the skin from your face. As often as I have had my werewolf brows waxed, I am still caught off guard every time. I have been unsuccessful in my attempts to convince myself that the pain will be worth it in the end. Kind of like that lie you tell yourself about childbirth. You know, the one about how once you see that beautiful baby, you instantaneously forget the pain. Yeah, right! I opted for epidurals when both my daughters were born and I don't understand why you can't get something similar when you get your eyebrows waxed.

LaVonda did an outstanding job with my brows. She gave me a mirror to inspect her work. Fabulous. Wolf woman was gone and Karen had reclaimed her face.

LaVonda wiped my brows with astringent to ease the throbbing and then she prepared me for what I thought was going to be a standard facial. She pulled my hair away from my face and wrapped it in a turban. As the calming music soothed me, natural fragrances engulfed my senses. I transitioned from a stressed, unkempt Superwoman to a relaxed, calm and chaos-free Karen.

In a soft and gentle voice, LaVonda said, "It is now time for your sensory journey." She presented me with three

It All Started When I Stopped Using Lotion

essential oils. The aromas were floral, oriental and citrus. I selected the light, oriental fragrance.

For the next forty-five minutes, LaVonda steamed my pores, cleaned my face and massaged my neck and shoulders. As a person who loves full-body massages, I never imagined that a facial would not only improve my complexion, but change my attitude and outlook on life. By far, that was the best facial I have ever had in my life! No exaggeration.

The sensory journey that I began while lying on a massage table at Square One Salon and Spa revealed something very important to me. When we invest a little bit of **TiME** in ourselves, the payoff is exponential. In the stock market, it is referred to as ROI: Return On Investment. If you are a woman who is committed to moving from chaos to calm, then you have the power to redefine PMS. From this point forward, when you say PMS, know that it means Pamper MySelf. And when you get to the point where you don't just say it, but you actually do it, just imagine the return on that investment.

I embrace PMS! How about you?

Karen M. R. Townsend, Ph.D.

Step Seven: 52 Ways to Take Your TiME

The first draft of this book included five steps and then there were six. The final product that you now hold in your hands has evolved into seven steps. Was this planned? Happenstance? A coincidence? Not at all. As a person who doesn't believe in coincidences, I believe that there are seven steps because seven is a significant number.

Think about it: There are seven seas, seven continents, and we often use the phrase "Seventh Heaven" to describe something as wonderful or spectacular. Those who study numerology equate the number seven with completion or perfection. Religious people acknowledge that after working tirelessly to create the world, on the seventh day, God rested. For you to move from chaos to calm, you too must take **TiME** to rest and to renew.

Before proceeding on this journey, I want to remind you of the first six steps.

Step One: Do Not Disturb

Set boundaries so that others will understand and respect your need for **TiME**.

Step Two: Joy!

Identify what brings you joy and develop a plan to incorporate those things into your life on a regular basis.

Step Three: Build a Chaos to Calm Team

Make a commitment to self-care and identify resources and support people who will reinforce your decision to make YOU a priority.

Step Four: Just say, "NO!"
To regain and maintain life balance, say "No!" to requests that drain your energy and consume too much of your **TiME**.

Step Five: Just Say, "YES!"
When you gain the courage to say "No!" to others, you create more opportunities to say "Yes!" to yourself.

Step Six: PMS
The real meaning of PMS is **P**amper **M**y**S**elf. From this day forward, you are committed to self-care and self-love. All of the indulgence. None of the guilt.

~ ~ ~ ~

After reading the previous chapters and completing the exercises and assessments, you may still struggle with identifying specific ways to take your **TiME**. You are clear as to why you need self-care and the positive affect it will have on your life. But you may be wondering, "What shall I do to care for myself?" Well, I have a few suggestions. Actually I have fifty-two: one for every week of the year. My hope is that eventually you will make a commitment to taking **TiME** every day. But until then, once a week is a great start. And please understand, I am still on this journey as well!

In our final step to move from chaos to calm, here are fifty-two options for your consideration. Some are self-explanatory. Others—especially the ones I particularly enjoy—include more detailed information. I encourage you to identify one activity that you will incorporate into your life **this week**. Next week, choose and implement another activity. Make this commitment a weekly habit and before you know it, you will discover that you are moving from chaos…to calm.

It All Started When I Stopped Using Lotion

52 Ways to Take Your TiME

1. **Spend the day at a spa.** One of my personal favorites. Nothing compares to spending the day in a soothing, serene environment and allowing someone to cater to you. When I want the ultimate PMS experience, I head to Square One in the Cannery District of Dayton, Ohio. Go on a quest to find your favorite spa and enjoy all the pampering in the process.
2. **Indulge in one service at a TiME.** If your budget will not allow you to spend an entire day at the spa, then do one service at a time. Start with a pedicure (this service changed my life) and then...
3. **Get a manicure.**
4. **Get a facial.**
5. **Get a massage.**
6. **High Tea.** High tea is an afternoon tradition started by the Brits in the early 1840s. The luxury began as a small meal of bread, butter, pastries and tea and later became a social activity with live entertainment. I recently learned that a local establishment offers high tea. Rather than the standard grab-and-go cup of coffee, cappuccino, espresso or latte, experience a beverage in a calm and peaceful setting. Unique Celebrations Tea Room in Centerville, Ohio is the perfect place to enjoy high tea. This tea room is dedicated to providing an atmosphere that makes drinking tea an occasion. Where can you go in your city to encounter a similar experience? Invite a girlfriend and have tea for two.

7. **Let someone else do your hair.** I'm sure that you are fully capable of operating a blow dryer and curling iron, but this week, let someone else do it. If you are really bold, try a new hairstyle!

8. **Take a bubble bath.** Another one on my list of favorite things. For far too long, I denied myself this simple pleasure. I am happy to report that bubble baths are once again part of my regular routine. It is simply amazing how much a soak in the tub can positively affect your life. Try it. You just might find that you love it!

9. **Take a bubble bath by candlelight.** Once you get into the habit of taking bubble baths, adding candlelight makes it an even more self-indulgent experience. Consider taking it to the next level by playing smooth jazz, grabbing a cool beverage and relaxing until your fingers and toes are wrinkly!

10. **Call in "well" to work.** Why is it that you never slow down or take a day off from work until you are sick? You push yourself and push yourself and push yourself some more, until finally you are sick. At that point, you have to stay home in bed for a day or two. Wouldn't it be nice to stay home from work when you we were feeling *good* instead of *bad*? Yes, you have two weeks of annual vacation, but sometimes you just need a day. If kids can play hooky from school, why can't you play hooky from work? So if you dare, call your boss and say, "I'm not coming in today. I'm just too darn well!"

11. **Make an appointment with an image consultant.** I envy women who always look like they just stepped out of the pages of *Vogue*. Their personal style and finesse carries with it an air of sophistication. Well, if you don't have a natural talent for style and fashion

(and I will be the first to admit that I do not) schedule time with a professional.

12. **Commune with nature.** You work inside. You live inside. You sit inside while you wait for your children at music and dance lessons. This week, go outside. Sit on your porch or spread a blanket in your backyard and enjoy the beauty of your surroundings.
13. **Take a hike.** Many communities have trails in beautiful wooded areas that provide a natural backdrop for a peaceful and serene walk. Put on your boots or sneakers and become one with nature.
14. **Express your creativity.** Have you convinced yourself that you are not creative? I did. Oh, the lies we tell ourselves! Even if you think you aren't creative, I challenge you to draw, paint, knit, crochet, cross-stitch or…. I am sure that at one point in your life, you tried one of these creative outlets. Regardless of whether you were good at it in the past, now is the **TiME** to try again!
15. **Go to a movie and treat yourself to the snacks that you really want.** While I don't want to be contradictory by encouraging you to make unhealthy life choices, every now and then a girl needs a vat of popcorn drowned in butter or a trough of tortilla chips drenched in a questionable substance commonly referred to as nacho cheese. Live dangerously and enjoy one (or both) of these treats. If you can't bring yourself to indulge in this decadence alone, invite a friend. But at least one time, be daring and go alone!
16. **Go to bed one hour earlier.** OMG! Just the thought of going to bed early gets me excited! How about you? If you are suffering from sleep deprivation, this strategy is the one and only cure!

17. **Get up one hour earlier.** Believe it or not, I find this technique very calming. When your house is quiet, use the opportunity to read, pray, meditate or write in your journal. What a way to start your day!
18. **Ask for help.** While asking for help is contrary to the code of conduct for Superwomen, by now, I hope you have retired your cape and stored it in a moth-proof, acid-free preservation box. (Warning: Unlike your wedding gown, you *are not* to pass this down to your daughter!) Understandably, you are probably often exhausted and overwhelmed because you try to do everything for everybody all the time! There is no shame in asking for help. Ask your husband or significant other. Ask your children. Ask your friends. Ask your neighbors. As the Bible says, "You have not because you ask not."
19. **Pay for help.** Yes, you read that right. At a time when economic recovery is on the hearts and minds of Americans, part of my duty as a patriotic American is to do what I can to spur employment. What better way to revitalize the economy than to pay for help? Because I work hard outside the home, sometimes the things inside the home don't get done. I used to feel guilty when my floors weren't sparkling clean like the ones on the television commercials. And the day I realized that there were no animated bubble men living in my toilet to make sure that it was always clean and disinfected, I was devastated! Then it came to me: why not pay for some help? It just makes sense. Help for you may come in the form of a babysitter who allows you to go on a date with that special someone or simply frees up your time so that you can take **TiME** to go to the spa. Help may be a housekeeper who comes every

other week to do those things that you just don't want to do (i.e. windows, floors and the toilets). Help may be a lady in your community who has retired from her first career and has now launched a business preparing meals for busy, working moms. Go ahead. Pay for some **TiME**.

20. **Go on a date...with yourself!** If you are single, this way is great for connecting with yourself. How can a life partner complement your life, if you don't know what you like? If you are married or in a long-term relationship, a solo date may provide a great opportunity for your to reconnect with yourself. If only for one night, you can have the date of your dreams—no compromises! Go to the movie that you want to see. Go the restaurant where you like to eat. Visit your favorite museum and linger at each exhibit, buy tickets to the opera or enjoy your favorite ballet without worrying if your date is bored. Learn to enjoy your own company!

21. **Go to a local park and swing away.** Remember when you were a little girl and you would swing and swing and swing? As an adult woman who is rapidly approaching fifty, I am not ashamed to admit that I still love to swing on a swing set. Many years ago, we purchased a top-of-the-line play set for our girls. As they grew older, they were less and less interested in swinging, climbing the rock wall or sliding down the sliding board. One day, when I looked out in the backyard in frustration because no one was using the swing set, I decided to go for swing. I planted my middle-aged bottom in the seat. I used my feet to push off from the ground. I pumped my legs up and down...and I swung and swung and swung. The blue

sky seemed to smile down at me. The wind blew through my hair. The sun kissed my face. It was a wonderful feeling! I have only one regret: not sliding down the sliding board!

22. **Celebrate YOUR holiday.** What do Martin Luther King, Jr., Christopher Columbus and St. Patrick all have in common? A holiday named in their honor. My sister said, "Your birthday is your special holiday given to you by God." From this year forward, treat your birthday as a national holiday and take the day off to celebrate.

23. **Send a card or handwritten note to a friend with whom you have been meaning to reconnect.** We live in an age that simplifies our ability to be in contact with others (i.e. voicemail, e-mail, text messages, instant messages, etc.), but we rarely do so on a personal level. What a treat it would be for your friend to receive mail that wasn't a bill. Who knows? If enough of us do this, we might reignite the concept of pen pals.

24. **Call a friend you haven't spoken to in while and take TiME to catch up.** As I wrote this, I recalled a wonderful conversation I had with a friend and sorority sister from college. It had been at least two years since Jean and I had spoken. Thanks to the persistence of Jackie—another sorority sister—Jean and I were able to reconnect. During our conversation, the three of us talked loudly, laughed uncontrollably and at one point, cried inconsolably. It was fantastic! I am sure that your life is very busy and you have so many things that you must do. But if you don't nurture your relationships, what is the point?

25. **Spend TiME with a friend you haven't connected with in a while.** Phone calls are great and writing letters is special, but sometimes we need to invest face time. My friend Shannon and I have known each other for almost thirty years. We live three hours from each other and as a result, we don't see each nearly enough. Recently, however, we came up with a novel idea: we had a friend-iversary. We spent the entire weekend together in Louisville, Kentucky—the city where we first met—and we celebrated twenty-eight years of friendship. If you can't spend an entire weekend with your friend, how about a day? On another occasion, Shannon and I met in the middle. She and I met in a central location which required that we only had to drive an hour and a half each. We had spa treatments, ate lunch and both made it back home by 5:00 PM. (This is a great example of what you can do when you call in well to work!)

26. **Spend an afternoon at a local bookstore.** Browse through the stacks and explore the written word. Kindles, Nooks and iPads are great, but nothing compares to holding a book in your hands. Today's bookstores have inviting atmospheres designed to encourage you to browse and sit a while. Take them up on the invitation.

27. **Spend the afternoon at a local museum.** Walk through the corridors and explore the artistic expressions. What do the pieces say to you? Be an art connoisseur and purchase a piece of art. If your budget won't allow you to purchase an expensive piece, visit the gift shop and buy postcards of works by your favorite artist.

28. **Spend the day at a water park or pool—without your children!** I did this once! I had so much fun riding down the Lazy River and didn't worry about where my children were or if they were in danger of drowning. And you haven't witnessed high comedy until you see a middle-aged woman squeal in delight as she plunges into the pool at the end of the waterslide!
29. **Walk in the snow.**
30. **Play in the snow.**
31. **Eat some snow.** Just make sure it isn't yellow!
32. **Play the piano, guitar or harp.**
33. **Take a nap.**
34. **Take a drive in the country.**
35. **Sit in a boat on a lake and pretend to fish.** I love this one! All the stress of catching a fish is eliminated because you're only pretending. Enjoy the benefits of the trip with no pressure to perform.
36. **Sit in a Jacuzzi and sip wine.** Disclaimer: DO NOT drink to intoxication! I do not wish to be held responsible if harm comes your way as a result of incorporating this strategy!
37. **Work in the garden.**
38. **Buy a coloring book, a box of Crayola Crayons and color.** Good news: unlike when we were kids, there will be no criticism if you color outside the lines.
39. **Go window shopping.** We don't always have to spend money at the mall to enjoy the experience.
40. **Keep your pajamas on all day and watch what you want on TV.** Just imagine…caressing the remote in your hand…all day long.
41. **Go to the DVD store and rent movies you want to see.** Buy movie candy, soda, a tub of microwave popcorn and spend the day watching movies at your

house. This strategy works well in pajamas. **Please note:** Change into your pajamas *after* returning from the DVD store.

42. **Visit a local florist and smell the roses.** Buy a bouquet of roses and have the salesperson write on the card, "I love you more than you know. Let this be the first of many days that you stop and smell the roses." Instruct the florist to put your name on the card as the recipient and have the flowers delivered to your home.
43. **Rest and think freely.**
44. **Take a field trip to the zoo, arboretum, gardens, etc.**
45. **Put your feet up and read a book.**
46. **Ride your bike.**
47. **Sing.**
48. **Take a yoga class.**
49. **Read the Bible, Torah, Koran or other spiritual book.** Initially, I only listed the Bible, but my intelligent daughter reminded me that while every woman is not a Christian, every woman should be encouraged to read a book that lifts her spirit.
50. **Do Nothing!** We always seem to be humans doing rather than humans being. For one moment in time, just be.
51. **Enjoy being with yourself, by yourself.** I learned this way from my introverted daughter. In her early teen years, I became concerned when I noticed that she didn't talk on the phone, have company over or go to friends' houses. After all, I am a social butterfly and she is my daughter. One day, I went into her room and asked about her friends and whether she was okay. She looked at me. With confidence and wisdom beyond her years, she said, "Mommy, I am fine. I enjoy my own

company." If only we could all be that content with ourselves.

And last but not least, if you can't think of anything else to do to take your **TiME**, then just

52. **Be still.** A few years back, I attended a conference with five sorority sisters. Rather than getting three separate rooms and doubling up, we pooled our money and booked a suite. It was awesome! We had two bedrooms, a kitchen and a huge living room for three whole days. No husbands. No children. No work. No responsibilities. On the first day, we had free time in the afternoon, so we gathered in our living room to watch *The Oprah Show*. I love the show, but typically do not get to watch it during the week (I DVR it to watch on the weekends...while folding laundry). My sisters and I laughed, talked and shared our personal thoughts about the topic of the day.

Then for no apparent reason, I jumped from the couch, grabbed the ironing board and began ironing my clothes.

Stacy, one sorority sister, looked at me in astonishment and asked, "What are you doing?"

"I'm ironing my clothes."

"We don't have to be anywhere for hours. Why are you doing that now?"

"I thought that since I'm watching television, I might as well do something."

Stacy looked at me with the wisdom of our ancestors and said, "That's not it. You just can't sit still."

Wow! Stacy had read me like a book. She was right. I couldn't sit still. I felt compelled to do, move, work or....

Jesus said, "Peace, be still."

It All Started When I Stopped Using Lotion

In that moment, when I just had to iron my clothes, I believe that Jesus sent a message through Stacy who challenged me to be still. I offer that challenge to you.

You cannot reach a place of peace or calm unless you are willing to be still.

Karen M. R. Townsend, Ph.D.

It All Started When I Stopped Using Lotion

Moving From Chaos to Calm

Reflect on the ***52 Ways to Take Your TiME***
and then answer the following questions:

Which strategy will you implement this week?

_____

_____

_____

_____

Why did you select this strategy?

_____

_____

_____

_____

How will this strategy bring more balance to your life?

_____

_____

_____

_____

Karen M. R. Townsend, Ph.D.

To assist you along your journey, I have provided a
*Take Your **TiME** Twelve-Week Calendar.*
List the strategy number, the date you plan to embark upon it
and the details including what, where and why.

Week	Strategy	Date	Details
1			
2			
3			
4			
5			
6			
7			
8			
9			
10			
11			
12			

It All Started When I Stopped Using Lotion

Final Thoughts

On Sunday, November 14, 2010, I, Karen M.R. Townsend took a bath.

Not just any bath: a bubble bath. Actually, it was more than a bubble bath because I took the opportunity to linger in the Jacuzzi for nearly an hour. I sipped an ice-cold glass of orange juice and because I can see my television from the bathtub, I watched *Desperate Housewives* as I soaked.

When my fingers and toes were wrinkly, I stepped out of the tub, dried off and then put on lotion! I didn't give it much thought, but it was the first time in a long time that I had experienced the bath-beverage-TV-lotion ritual. I was amazed at the effect of this in-home PMS experience. I was calmer than I had been in a long while. In the days following, I was more loving to my husband and children, more engaged with my friends and more productive on my job. I was more giving in my community, happier with myself than I had been in years and I was able to finally finish this book!

What made the difference? What caused the turnaround? What turned me into the woman who felt loved and appreciated and as a result was able to give love and appreciation to others?

Well, I'm not 100% sure because I have no empirical evidence. I have not conducted a research study or consulted with experts, but here is what I think may have sparked the turnaround...

All the stress...
All the turmoil...
All the craziness...
All the chaos...
All the drama...

It all STOPPED when I STARTED using lotion!

I had come full circle. During the period when I denied myself the modest pleasure of lotion—a metaphor that now represents balance in my life—I lived a stress-filled, chaotic existence. Now, however, as the result of a journey that took years, I have reached the destination that I almost believed would forever elude me: a state of calm.

After one bubble bath and one application of lotion, KT was back! Back with a renewed commitment to setting boundaries. Back to making self-care a part of my regular routine. Back to making myself a priority.

My, oh my! What a little lotion will do!

Wherever you are on your journey from chaos to calm, may you always take **TiME** to put on lotion!

Next Steps: Opportunities to Apply Lotion

As you begin—or continue—your journey from chaos to calm, I offer these resources to expedite your trip. While some of the people, places and things are unique to my hometown of Dayton, Ohio, they provide ideas of the types of resources to look for in your community. Remember, lotion is a metaphor for the little things we do to bring balance, joy, and calm into our lives. I encourage you to find your own opportunities to apply lotion.

Sometimes the greatest resources come from people like you! If you have resources to share or stories of your journey from chaos to calm, I would love to hear from you. Email me at KT@AboutMySisters.com.

People
Karen S. Waugh, LISW-S; LICDC-CS
Waugh Counseling Services
3805 North High Street Suite 310
Columbus, Ohio 43214
614.664.6010

Karen M. R. Townsend, Ph.D.

I have often told my stressed-out friends and professional colleagues that I knew I had finally arrived when I had to retain the services of a licensed professional counselor! To quote my sister, Etene Terrell, "Everyone deserves a couch trip now and then." Seriously, no shame exists in seeking the assistance of a professional who can provide a listening ear and offer objective advice. For many years, Loretta Murphy in Dayton, Ohio served this purpose in my life—and I am forever grateful for her sage wisdom. When she retired in 2012, I went in search of a new therapist. My sister offered the recommendation: Karen Waugh. Karen believes in self-determination and choice as a part of the natural process of growth. For me, this knowledge has meant that I must be an active participant in becoming the ME I say I want to be. In collaboration with Karen the therapist, this Karen (ME!) had to accept not only her support, but her honest feedback. If you live in Central Ohio and need a therapist, Karen is the one to get. And if you don't live in Central Ohio, after the initial in-person consultation, you can reach her by Skype!

Wanda J. Corner, Ph.D. Executive Business Coach
Corner of Success, Inc.
CornerOfSuccessInc.biz
PO Box 18429
Atlanta, Georgia 30316
404.622.3944

Talk about holding someone accountable! After interviewing me, Dr. Corner agreed to be my executive coach. She assisted me in clarifying goals in all areas of my life, while helping me get a clear picture of what I want for my future. We often compartmentalize our lives. Coach Wanda taught me that I exist as a multi-faceted being: wife,

It All Started When I Stopped Using Lotion

mother, educator, entrepreneur, speaker, trainer, consultant and now author. Harmonious co-existence while wearing all those hats is possible, but sometimes we need a coach to show us how. If you have ever considered a coach—which is different from a counselor or a therapist—I highly recommend Coach Wanda. She offers her services virtually, so no matter where you are, her services are available. Coach Wanda is dedicated to "coaching and motivating people and organizations to success."

Places to Relax
Square One Salon and Day Spa
SquareOneSalon.com
506 East Third Street
Dayton, Ohio 45402
937.461.2222

Hands down and without a doubt, Square One is my favorite place for a PMS experience! Whether you are booking a single service or an entire day, Brent and his team have what it takes to move you from chaos to calm.

Skyline Chili
SkylineChili.com

My youngest daughter, KaeLyn, reminded me that my favorite food is chili dogs. When I don't make them at home, I buy them at Skyline. I had no intention of listing a restaurant as a resource, but sometimes all it takes to change my mood is a coney dog covered with chili, cheese, beans and onions!

Unique Celebrations Gift Shop and Tea Room
UniqueCelebrationShop.com
33 West Franklin Street
Centerville, Ohio 45459
937.434.7467

While "high tea" began as a British tradition, it is no longer an experience reserved only for those residing in the United Kingdom. This tea room is a delightful place to spend an afternoon with your girlfriends, your mom or your daughters. Owned and operated by mother-daughter team Kathy and Samantha Jablinski, this tea room also offers "unique" gifts and party items. I was particularly impressed with the assortment of hats which they invite visitors to don while sipping tea!

Places to Write
As I worked to finish this book, I found that I was more productive when I worked remotely. The places that I visited frequently were

Panera Bread
PaneraBread.com

Boston Stoker
BostonStoker.com

It All Started When I Stopped Using Lotion

Things to Do

Visit AboutMySisters.com to learn more about our programs which are dedicated to the growth and development of women and girls. Through workshops, seminars, conferences and retreats, our mission is to educate, inform and enlighten women and girls to discover their unique talents and abilities. When we have the confidence to recognize and embrace our power, the result will be a generation of women and girls living up to their maximum potential.

Review online information about the following events:
- Retreats for Renewal
- I'M POSSIBLE: An Empowerment Program for Adolescent Girls
- The SisterCircle
- The SisterCruise
- Breakthrough to You: A One-Day Empowerment Program for Women
- Sister to Sister: An African American Women's Think Tank

Books to Read
- *Patches of Inspiration* by Sonie Bigbee
- *Uncommon Sense: For Real Women in the Real World* by Suzette Brawner and Jill Brawner Jones
- *Sacred Pampering Principles* by Debrena Jackson Gandy
- *Wit and Wisdom for Women* by Barbara Jenkins
- *I'm Here, Now What? A Woman's Guide In Corporate America* by Toni Perry Gillispie
- *Keynotes* by Stacey Lawson
- *The Frazzled Female: 30 Days to Finding God's Peace In Your Daily Chaos* by Cindy Wood

Karen M. R. Townsend, Ph.D.

It All Started When I Stopped Using Lotion

About the Author

Karen M.R. Townsend, Ph.D. is president and CEO of KTownsend Consulting, an Ohio-based training and consulting firm offering expertise in leadership development, 21st-century diversity issues and personal excellence. With a career spanning more than twenty-five years, Dr. Townsend serves clients in educational institutions, government agencies, major corporations and non-profit organizations.

Dr. Townsend has a passion for creating innovative programs for women and girls. In 1993, she hosted the first SISTER TO SISTER Conference with colleagues Lillian Johnson and Charlotta Taylor. This conference—designed to provide a forum for the personal and professional development of women—is one of the longest running women's conferences in the Miami Valley (Ohio) region. In 2010, Dr. Townsend launched About My Sisters (AboutMySisters.com)—an organization dedicated to the growth and empowerment of women and girls.

Dr. Townsend is a graduate of Kentucky State University, The Ohio State University and the University of Dayton. She is a member of Alpha Kappa Alpha Sorority, Inc., Toastmasters International and Tabernacle Baptist Church. Dr. Townsend is an active community volunteer and has served on the boards of numerous non-profit organizations. She was featured in the Cincinnati/Dayton *SuccessGuide* in recognition of her professionalism, commitment to community service and volunteerism. In 2010, Dr. Townsend was named a "Woman of Influence" by the Dayton YWCA and one of the "25 Women to Watch" by Women in Business Networking.

Dr. Townsend resides in Dayton, Ohio with her husband, Sylvester J. Townsend, Jr. and their daughters, Syron and KaeLyn.

Karen M. R. Townsend, Ph.D.

Training and Consulting

Dr. Townsend is available to lead programs for educational institutions, corporations, associations, conventions and public seminars. Her most requested topics include

Personal Excellence

- Personal Strategic Planning: Creating An Action Plan for Your Success
- Get a Life!: Balancing Your Life While Building Your Career
- The Who vs. The Do: Understanding the Difference Between What You Do and Who You Are

Leadership Development

- Leadership: From Rhetoric to Reality
- What's Your Style?: Discovering and Defining How You Function as A Leader
- Coaching to Win: A Leader's Game Plan for Success

21st-Century Diversity

- Inclusive Leadership: Leveraging Diversity for Organizational Success
- Awareness101: Valuing Diversity in the Workplace
- Silents, Boomers, Gen X'ers and Beyond: How to Balance the Generations At Work

Each presentation is customized to meet the unique goals and objectives of the client.

For more information on these and other programs, contact Dr. Townsend at 937.602.4641 or email KTownsend@Consultant.com.

It All Started When I Stopped Using Lotion

Queen V Publishing
The Doorway to YOUR Destiny!

*Go thou and publish abroad
the kingdom of God.*
—Luke 9:60

We are a contract publisher committed to transforming manuscripts into polished works of art. **Queen V Publishing**, a company of standard and integrity, offers an alternative that allows the message in YOU to do what it was sent to do for OTHERS.

Visit the website for complete guidelines on manuscript submission and the plan that best fits your literary goals.

QueenVPublishing.com
We help experts master self-publishing!

Valerie J. Lewis Coleman
Dayton, Ohio

Karen M. R. Townsend, Ph.D.

Other Queen V Titles…

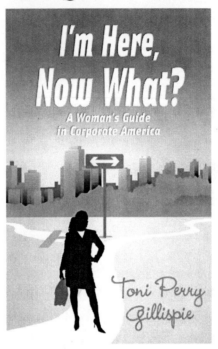

Are you tired of fighting your way to the top?

Climbing the ladder of Corporate America may sometimes feel like you're moving sideways. In *I'm Here Now What?*, Toni Perry Gillispie's expert guidance will help you choose the best path for you and encourage you to enjoy the journey.

Through life applications, self-evaluations and sprinkles of affirmations, you will learn how to shatter the glass ceiling.

TheInspiredWord.net

Also available on Amazon.com
ISBN-13: 978-0-9817436-3-9
$9.95 US

It All Started When I Stopped Using Lotion

Pen of the Writer

*Out of Ephraim was there a root of them against Amalek; after thee, Benjamin, among thy people; out of Machir came down governors, and out of Zebulun they that handle the **pen of the writer**.*
~ Judges 5:14

Pen Of the WritER

is a Christian publishing company committed to using the writing pen as a weapon to fight the enemy and celebrate the good news of Christ Jesus.

With over ten years of experience, Pen of the Writer prides itself on providing literary services for novice writers and published authors including

Queen V Publishing
Passionate Pens
Writing and Publishing Conferences
Coaching and Consultation
Self-Publishing Made Easy

Pen of the Writer
Taking writers from pen to paper to published!

Pen of the Writer, LLC
Dayton, Ohio
PenOfTheWriter.com

Karen M. R. Townsend, Ph.D.

The Forbidden Secrets of the Goody Box
What your father didn't tell you and your mother didn't know
By Valerie J. Lewis Coleman

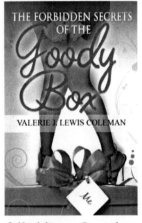

Successful. Beautiful. Intelligent. Yet a satisfying relationship eludes Debra Hampton. At thirty-five years old, she can't figure out why her philosophy on men—and what they want from women—isn't working. She's trapped in a cycle of shattered relationships, until a friend refers her to a relationship guru. After some resistance, Debra finds refuge in his counsel as he helps her navigate through the storms of rejection and failed love. Once he reveals the error of her ways, will Debra master the forbidden secrets to attract her soul mate or continue to keep love at bay? **TheGoodyBoxBook.com**

Blended Families An Anthology
An Amazon.com Bestseller!
By Valerie L. Coleman

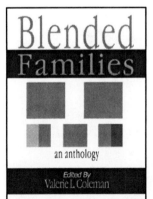

With divorce, single-parent households and family crises on the rise, many people are experiencing the tumultuous dynamics of blended or stepfamilies. Learn biblical principles and practical tools to help your family thrive. ***Blended Families An Anthology*** ministers to the needs of those hurting and crying out for answers.

Available in paperback and e-book on **Amazon.com.com** and **PenOfTheWriter.com**

It All Started When I Stopped Using Lotion

For speaking engagements or to order additional copies of

It All Started When I Stopped Using Lotion

About My Sisters
PO Box 111
Clayton, OH 45315
AboutMySisters.com
Info@AboutMySisters.com

* * * * * * * * * * * * * * * * *

Please mail _____ copies of

It All Started When I Stopped Using Lotion

Name _____

Address _____

City / State / Zip _____

(_____) _____
Phone

Email _____

Quantity	Price Per Book	Total
	$12.95	
Sales Tax (Ohio residents add $0.91 per book)		
Shipping ($3.49 first book, $0.99 each additional)		
Grand Total* (Payable to: About My Sisters)		

* Certified check and money orders only

Also Available on Amazon.com

Karen M. R. Townsend, Ph.D.

CPSIA information can be obtained at www.ICGtesting.com
Printed in the USA
BVOW05s0720210414

351169BV00001B/67/P